The Enchanted Land

6

THE ENCHANTED LAND

Myths and Legends
of Britain's Landscape

Janet and Colin Bord

Thorsons
An Imprint of HarperCollins*Publishers*

Thorsons
An Imprint of HarperCollins*Publishers*
77–85 Fulham Palace Road,
Hammersmith, London W6 8JB
1160 Battery Street,
San Francisco, California 94111–1213

Published by Thorsons 1995
1   3   5   7   9   10   8   6   4   2

A catalogue record for this book is available from the British Library

ISBN 1 85538 407 8

Printed in Ehrhardt by HarperCollinsManufacturing Glasgow

Contents

Introduction

This book has its origins in a visit to the Drake Stone in Northumberland (*see Chapter 7 and Places to Visit*) – or rather a return visit, for Colin and I first visited it some years ago while researching one of our earlier books. Now I was revisiting it in the company of good friends, at the end of a week spent touring the ancient places of Northumberland and Durham, and it affected me again as it had done the first time, fuelling the flames of my enthusiasm for those mystical places in the landscape that have had a significance in people's lives.

The Drake Stone, dominating the hill by Harbottle and attainable only after a stiff climb, is a good example of a once-widespread interaction between people and the landscape, in its use as a curative site. Parents would pass their sickly children over the top of the stone to effect a cure: not too difficult, you might think, but it is a very tall and forbidding stone and the procedure must have been dangerous. The participants in this apparently (to us) pointless ritual must have had a strong belief in its efficacy, but why did they believe in it? Thoughts of the people driven to try such a procedure, their toil up the hill carrying a sick child, their struggle to perform the ritual correctly, their hopes of success . . . this was my starting point, and from this human involvement with the landscape arose the idea for *The Enchanted Land*, a book devoted solely to the folklore and legend of natural landscape features in Britain.

Britain's rich legacy of folklore was originally handed down by word of mouth from one generation to the next, and fortunately a number of folklore collectors during the last century wrote down those tales that were still remembered. Since the First World War and especially with the development of radio and television, the art of story-telling has died, and so most of the folklore would have been lost with the deaths of the last people who held it in their memories, had it not been collected and written down. So it is fortunate that we do still have a rich collection of folklore material accessible in written form, though there is no knowing how much material has been lost through not having been collected and written down in time. We gathered our material from many such folklore collections, the most useful ones being listed in the bibliography.

Since this book concentrates on the folklore and legend of natural landscape features in Britain, we have ignored all man-made structures, from prehistoric standing stones onwards, and concentrated solely on hills and mountains, rivers and streams, caves and hollows, springs and wells, cliffs and coasts, pools and lakes, and rocks and stones. Occasionally there may be some inadvertent overlap, in that a hill may have been used as the site for a fort or castle, a cave may have been lived in or worked as a mine, a stone may have been placed in position by prehistoric men rather than being moved there by natural forces. But by and large the majority of sites we write about are wholly natural. Similar tales and legends have also grown up around man-made structures, of course, and details of some of those relating to prehistoric sites will be found in our earlier book *The Secret Country*.

As is usually clear from their fantastic nature, a large proportion of the tales in this book are pure invention with no factual basis whatsoever. But some are more ambiguous, and may have been founded on fact. These include the accounts of drowned lands, and the formation of holy wells, for instance. Some long-held folklore beliefs may have been survivals from early, pre-Christian religions: that rivers have spirits that demand sacrifices, for example. To isolate the original stimulus from the changes and distortions that have accumulated as a story or belief or ritual has been passed down through the generations is probably impossible: the wheat has become so intermixed with the chaff that to separate the two is now beyond our skill. Any person who attempts it cannot avoid being influenced by his or her own beliefs, and therefore the folklore cannot be interpreted with any guarantee of impartiality.

So we must confess our uncertainty as to the ultimate value of these tales as sources of ancient wisdom. Having said that, there is no doubt that many of the places we describe do have powerful atmospheres and are evocative of the hidden and mysterious aspects of Britain's past. Readers are free to interpret the tales for themselves, and to usefully extract whatever nuggets of wisdom seem appropriate to them.

The final section of the book is a fuller description of some of the most interesting sites that are worth visiting. We give full details of the folklore that has survived, and information on where the sites are located, including Ordnance Survey map references where relevant, to make them easier to find. Any site in Chapters 1–7 with * after its name will be found in *Places to Visit*. Throughout we have given county names for sites, using the present county names for England and Wales, and the old county names in Scotland, because there the post-1975 regions are sometimes very large.

Most of the photographs were taken by us, except for the following: Suilven, witch-burning site, Storr Pinnacles by Hamish Brown; St Sidwell by Roy Fry. All the photographs are held in the Fortean Picture Library.

JANET BORD
Clwyd, December 1993

3

Hills and Mountains

The wild uplands of Britain are mysterious places, distant, inaccessible, sometimes wreathed in mist. No wonder that they were often peopled with giants, fairies, ghosts and other fearsome beings, and considered to be places best avoided. The activities of giants, or sometimes the Devil, were held to be responsible for the formation of hills that are prominent in the landscape, while some unusual-shaped mountains in Scotland, especially Quinag, Suilven and the Stack, in Sutherland, were said to have been formed by the Norse gods when they were practising forming mountains.

Perhaps the best-known English hill formed by giants is The Wrekin* in Shropshire. In one version it began as a spadeful of earth being carried by a giant who intended to destroy Shrewsbury, but he gave up and dropped it before reaching the town because he was misled by a quick-witted cobbler into believing he still had a long way to walk. He then scraped his boots, and that pile of soil became Ercall Hill close by. Rocks scattered on top of hills were sometimes left there by giants, like the rocky summit of Bosley Cloud which was a giant's shoe: a

5

giant king who stood with one foot on the Cloud and the other on Shutlingsloe near Wildboarclough (Cheshire) left his shoe behind as he stepped off. Again in Shropshire, the rocks on top of Titterstone Clee were left after a battle between giants, and they surround the so-called Giant's Chair. A prominent rock on top of a hill was often described as a chair or seat, and the name of a mountain in north-west Wales, Cadair Idris, actually means Idris's chair: Idris was a local giant, the chief of four giants whose names are still those of mountains around Dolgellau (Gwynedd). It was said that anyone who stayed in Idris's chair overnight would next morning be found dead, raving mad, or a genius.

The famous historical (or legendary?) King Arthur was sometimes seen as a giant figure. He had several seats or chairs, one in Devon, one between the two highest peaks of the Brecon Beacons (Powys), one on King's Crags at Sewingshields (Northumberland), and one of course at Tintagel* (Cornwall) where he was said to have been born. There no doubt others, as there are also several sites which claim to be his Round Table. Most of those are either prehistoric or later structures, and so do not qualify for inclusion in this book, but one is possibly a natural feature, and that is Bwrdd Arthur (Arthur's Table in Welsh), near Llansannan (Clwyd), where on a rocky hillside is a rough circle of hollows. The Devil too has his chairs, one being on the highest point of the Stiperstones* (Shropshire), where he sat one day when he was carrying an apron full of stones to fill Hell Gutter. Another of his chairs is on Largo Law, a rocky hill in Fife. In fact the hill itself was a lump of rock dropped by the Devil.

The Devil must have been a busy chap, carrying around loads of stones and earth, because a considerable number of hills throughout Britain were formed as a result of his activities. The Devil's Spadeful near Bewdley (Worcestershire) shows him in vindictive mood, planning to bury Bewdley under a load of earth, until he met a cobbler on the road who showed him his bag of worn-out shoes and said he had worn them all out since walking from Bewdley. In disgust the Devil dropped his load and gave up. But he tried the same trick again elsewhere, for example in Hertfordshire where he intended to bury Stevenage. He threw soil from a hole he had dug, but it fell short and the seventh spadeful, after knocking the spire off Graveley church, formed a small hill close by. In Herefordshire two hills called Robin Hood's Butts have a similar origin, when the Devil was planning to bury Hereford but was persuaded not to by a holy man in disguise who told him that the people of the city were too wicked to waste his time on. As the name of these two hills suggests, another version of the tale had Robin Hood as the giant figure with evil intent, and his intention was to bury the monks at Wormesley. Meon Hill in Warwickshire was also once a missile against a religious community, for the Devil threw it in the direction of Evesham Abbey. The lump of earth was stopped in flight by the prayers of St Egwin, and it dropped harmlessly to the ground.

Loads of stone which the Devil accidentally dropped include How Hill at Ludham (Norfolk), one of several piles of gravel scattered by him in this area; while Dunkery Hill, the highest point of Exmoor (Somerset/Devon), is composed of rock and soil he dumped there while digging out the large hole on Winsford Hill known as the Punchbowl. The Devil's Bag of Nuts is an unusually named hill near Alcester (Warwickshire), so-called because it was the result of his labours on the Devil's Nutting Day (21 September). Unfortunately for him, no sooner had he gathered a bagful of nuts than he met the Virgin Mary, and the shock caused him to throw down his bag before rushing away. Torbery Hill (Sussex) also resulted from the Devil's discomfiture: he burnt his mouth sipping hot punch from a spoon he had dipped into his Punch Bowl in Surrey, and in pain he flung the spoon away. This giant-sized utensil became Torbery Hill.

Sometimes already existing hills were torn apart to form the shapes that we can now see today. One notable example is the three prominent peaks of the Eildon Hills* (Roxburgh) which were originally joined to form one hill, until split by a group of devils on the orders of the wizard Michael Scot. Adam's Rocks in Herefordshire were torn apart at the Crucifixion, and a cleft in the side of Skirrid, Gwent's holy mountain, was likewise formed during an earthquake which heralded Christ's death. An alternative explanation for this feature is that the famous local wizard, Jack o' Kent, left his heel mark on Skirrid when he jumped from another hill, the Sugar Loaf, nearby. More prosaically, a furrow in the Clent Hills (Worcestershire) was formed when the oxen pulling an old woman's plough ran away in protest at being made to work on St Kenelm's Day (or alternatively, she started to plough on a Sunday, was struck blind, and her oxen escaped).

The religious connection continues in the stories of how two small hills were formed. One at Llanddewi Brefi (Dyfed) rose up where St David stood to preach, so that he could be heard by the whole multitude of people who had gathered to listen. To the north in Scotland, a hill near Hoddom Castle north-west of Annan (Dumfries) rose up at the place where St Kentigern, a seventh-century monk, bishop and evangelist (who was the same as St Mungo, Glasgow's patron) met Rhydderch ap Tudwal, ruler of the kingdom of Strathclyde, in 573. The hill rose up so that the crowds could witness this momentous event.

Grassy hills and rocky mountains, even those with formation legends such as we have described, look harmless enough to the innocent eye, but what might they conceal inside? Larger-than-life figures of history and legend are sometimes said to live – or sleep – inside hills such as Torvean close to Inverness, where Lady Macbeth is said to be imprisoned, though unable to sleep. A boy herding goats on the hill, awoke at dusk from a sleep, and heard light footsteps like that of a woman walking endlessly back and forth. She is sometimes still seen washing her hands in the River Ness nearby. She scrubs at them with leaves from a tree, or stones from the riverbed, and also paces slowly up and down. Merlin, the magician of Arthurian legend, is imprisoned inside Merlin's Hill on the outskirts of Carmarthen (Dyfed). At twilight his groans can be heard, and the clanking of the chains that hold him. He doubtless bewails his folly in falling in love with Vivien and teaching her the magic rituals she then used to imprison him. From a 'chair' on top of the hill he is said to have delivered his prophecies.

Blencathra, a hill in Cumbria, is one of many places where King Arthur is said to lie sleeping, with his knights and horses, awaiting the call to aid Britain in her hour of need. As the sleeping heroes are usually inside a cave in the hill or rock which conceals them, many more examples will be given in Chapter 3, Caves and Hollows. Sometimes the beings concealed inside hills are not sleeping or imprisoned, but dead. The Devil is apparently buried inside Windwhistle (Somerset), having died of the cold during a severe winter. In Haldon Hill, Kenford (Devon), a giant is said to be buried, his grave marked by two stones at head and foot, though they are a long distance apart. The exact distance is unknown, for it was said that it could not be measured.

Trencrom Hill*, an atmospheric rocky hill in Cornwall not far from St Ives, was the home of giants who kept their treasure there, guarded by spriggans, ugly fairies who could change size at will, and may have been giants' ghosts. A man who thought he knew where the treasure was hidden, began to dig in the hill one night, but a terrifying storm blew up, and in the flashes of lightning he saw the spriggans coming out of the rocks, getting larger all the time. He fled in terror, and was unable to work for a very long time. Numerous other hills are also said to be the hiding place of buried treasure, including Moel Arthur in the Clwydian Hills (Clwyd). The exact spot is marked by lights, but anyone who tries to dig there will be scared off by an almighty storm. Also in Clwyd, a great treasure was said to be buried at Bwrdd Ar·hur (the King Arthur's Table mentioned earlier), but a storm blows up if anyone tries to dig for it. In another version, a large chamber in the hill is filled with gold, guarded by a mighty sword hanging over the entrance, which will fall on anyone who tries to enter. The treasure, said to be buried at Broomfield in the Quantock Hills (Somerset), is equally hard to steal, being guarded by spirits whose groans frighten away even the most hardened thief. One man did manage to find the door to the stronghold and took a servant and tools with him, but the servant was nearly pulled inside by the spirits, until his master put a Bible on his head and dragged him away. The elusive door closed tight and changed its location so that no one else could find it. Occasionally hidden treasure can be found, but it must be the right person who finds it. One day a little girl playing on Pentyrch, a hill above Llangybi (Gwynedd), touched a large stone and it moved. Previously this stone could not be moved by anyone, even when they tried using horses to pull it. All these people were after the treasure believed to be hidden under the stone, but it was the little girl who found it, because she was the right one: her parents were at that time in desperate need of money.

We have seen that legendary figures like King Arthur and Merlin are said to live in some hills, and hidden treasure and giants are also associated with them, but the beings who are most often believed to live inside hills and mountains are the fairyfolk or Little People. Sometimes the tales are simply legends, like that from the fifteenth century describing the meeting between Thomas the Rhymer (Thomas of Erceldoune) and the Fairy Queen on the Eildon Hills* (Roxburgh): she led him inside the hills to her home in fairyland, where he stayed for three years before emerging as a poet and prophet. Sometimes the tales have a more recent and factual basis, such as the experience reported in August 1862 by David Evans and Evan Lewis, who were returning home through Carmarthenshire (Dyfed) and stopped with their horses and waggons at Cwmdwr in the early afternoon. There were men reaping a cornfield close by, and as the two men were looking at a hillside not far away, they saw what they first thought were about fifty small stacks of wheat. But they began to move, so perhaps they were reapers, the men thought. As the two watched, the 'reapers', who were all dressed alike, climbed a winding footpath and on reaching a level place on the hill, began to dance in a circle. After a short while they all disappeared into the ground; then they reappeared and began to dance again, before finally vanishing. When the two men met an old man on the road, they asked him about the men they had seen dancing in a circle, and he told them that he had heard his grandfather say that the Tylwyth Teg (fairies) had used to dance on the hill. Although this account dates from over a hundred years ago, similar sights are still reported today, and the people who see the fairies are as normal as you or me.

Some of the hills which have in the past been connected with the fairyfolk are: Fairy Hill, Aberfoyle* (Perth), where in the seventeenth century the Reverend Robert Kirk was said to have been taken to Fairyland inside the hill; Dinas Bran*, Llangollen (Clwyd), where a man joined them in a dance and could not stop; Kennavarra Hill in Tiree (Inner Hebrides) where two children, out to look at a snare one moonlit winter's night, heard wonderful music coming from below the ground; and Bearey Mountain (Isle of Man) where a man saw 'multitudes of the good people . . . wending their way up the side of the hill until they were lost in the mist . . .' They wore red pointed caps and carried various domestic articles like pots and pans, and it was presumed that they were seeking new quarters, having been disturbed by the noise of a new fulling mill. Fairies have also been seen on Bedwellty Mountain (Gwent), where a man travelling alone at night saw them dancing and heard a bugle blown as if they were about to start hunting. Remembering that they would disappear if a knife were shown, he drew his and they vanished.

The fairies were very fond of dancing, and their favourite dancing grounds included: the mountain Aran Fawddwy and the hillsides between Aber Rhiwlech and Bwlch y Groes nearby (Gwynedd), where one summer evening a boy saw them dancing and had to run to escape the entreaties of two fairy maidens who tried to persuade him to join them; Freni Fawr in the Prescelly Mountains near Cardigan (Dyfed) where a shepherd boy did join the fairy ring and then found himself in an elegant palace, only returning home years later, though he thought he had been absent but minutes; Moel Famau in the Clwydian Hills, and Craig Bron Bannog on Hiraethog (both in Clwyd). All these places must also have been entrances to Fairyland, and there were other locations where it was said that such a doorway existed. Among these was Mellor Moor near Blackburn in Lancashire, where an underground city was believed to exist, it having been swallowed up by an earthquake, but presumably this underground city was Fairyland since the fairies were said to parade in military dress on the mountainsides: one man, a relative of the man who wrote down his story, claimed to have seen a 'dwarf-like man, attired in full hunting costume, with top-boots and spurs, a green jacket, red hairy cap, and a thick hunting whip in his hand' running quickly across the moor, jumping a low stone wall, and then being lost to sight. Rocky Craig-y-Ddinas* in the Vale of Neath (West Glamorgan) was a fairy stronghold, said to be the place where they held their last court in Wales (*see plate 3*); and on Hackpen Hill (Wiltshire) also, the fairies were seen. A shepherd told how the ground had opened and he had been taken underground to strange places where music was played.

A fairy queen ruled the underground palace of Tom-na-hurich*, the Hill of the Yews near Inverness; but the best-known account of a doorway into fairyland concerns Glastonbury Tor* (Somerset), that powerful hill standing high above the Somerset Levels and focal point for so many strange tales. Here at Glastonbury was Annwn, the Celtic Underworld, and its lord was Gwyn ap Nudd, king of the fairies. St Collen, a sixth-century wandering saint, was living as a hermit on the Tor when he heard two men speaking about Gwyn. He warned them not to speak of devils, and they told him that Gwyn would send for him. Indeed he did, sending a messenger to Collen's cell, but the saint refused the invitation on three occasions. Finally he agreed to go, but hid a flask of holy water in his cloak. He was taken through a secret door into the hill, and saw Gwyn sitting on a golden chair in a palace. Collen refused to eat the fairy food that was offered to him, not wishing to find himself in their power. He sprinkled holy water all around, and was immediately alone on the hillside.

The fairy inhabitants of hills and mountains often interacted with the humans who lived close by, though such interaction was not always welcome. A fairy sprite known as a loireag, who haunted Ben More on South Uist (Outer Hebrides) was dreaded because she and her fellows were fond of milk, and would put a spell on the goats and cows grazing on the slopes of the mountain. She was even seen sucking at a cow's udder in broad daylight, and didn't stop when sworn at. The crofter then threw a stone at her, but again she ignored him. So he touched the tip of one of the cow's horns, saying the name of St Columba, and the loireag jumped away and ran screaming up the hillside, cursing the crofter and his cow. But the fairies could sometimes be helpful. In Sussex the fairies of Beeding Hill rescued a pig belonging to a farmer who had kept on good terms with them.

The fairyfolk are not the only denizens to haunt the hills of Britain. Witches and dragons can be found there too, if you know where to look. You could also encounter the Devil, the Wild Hunt, and the ghosts of humans and animals: hills and mountains are spooky places to be, especially on a foggy winter's night . . .

One of the Dartmoor tors, Vixen Tor close by Merrivale Bridge (Devon), was the haunt of an evil witch whose pleasure it was to cause mist to fall, misleading travellers so that they died in the bogs. But one man who had a magic ring given him by the pixies, which made him invisible, put it on and was able to push her off the rocks into the bog below. Many hills and mountains in Wales were said to be witch haunts, the places where they met together to dance and hatch their mischievous plans. Just a few of those places were the Clwydian Hills, Hiraethog and the Berwyns (Clwyd),Cadair Idris, Snowdon, and Mynydd Mawr (Gwynedd), the Breiddin, Long Mountain, and the Kerry Hills (Powys), and also many South Wales hills, such as the Prescellies (Dyfed). In England too there were in all counties certain locations where witches were believed to gather, but the most famous hill in this context must be Pendle Hill* in Lancashire, focal point for witchcraft in the area during the sixteenth century.

Legendary witches were usually thought of as evil, up to no good, though in fact many witches were 'white' witches with healing skills and a special knowledge of plants and animals. Because of the secretive nature of witchcraft, it is impossible to be sure just how widely it was really practised, and how much was black and how much white. The same applies today, and the same suspicion hangs over any mention of witchcraft, though the rituals are frequently innocent in their intentions. In 1945 a murder took place that still remains officially unsolved, though because of the way it had been carried out it was said to have been a ritual witch-slaying. The victim was an elderly farm labourer, Charles Walton, who sixty years earlier in 1885 had seen a phantom black dog nine times on Meon Hill (Warwickshire), close to the village of Lower Quinton where he lived. Because of this experience, and his ability with animals and birds, and the fact that he carried a piece of dark glass – a witch's mirror? – with him, and probably other reasons besides, Walton was locally thought to be involved in witchcraft and the occult. He died while out hedge-trimming on Meon Hill: he was found pinned to the ground by his pitchfork, its two tines on either side of his neck and driven 6 inches deep into the ground. He had been slashed with his sharp billhook, and it was left stuck into his chest, where a rough cross had been cut.

The local police found the case a difficult one to solve, and the famous Superintendent Fabian of Scotland Yard was called in. While out on the hill, he saw a large black dog, whether real or phantom is not now clear, but people were more than ever convinced that witchcraft was involved in the case. The death occurred on 14 February, Candlemas according to the old calendar, a witchcraft festival. The victim's blood had run directly into the soil and he was pinned to the ground. Was this a ritual sacrifice intended to both destroy Walton's evil influence and to fertilize the land? The witchcraft theory has never been proved, and the murder could have been for other reasons, simply being arranged to look as though witchcraft was involved and thus deflect the police from the motive and thence from the killer. People who have studied the case closely, including Fabian, believed that Alfred Potter, the farmer who employed Walton, was the killer, but it could not be proved, and also the motive remains unclear.

What is certain is that witchcraft's bad reputation resulted in a great many murders of genuine or more probably imagined witches. Echoes of these cruel practices have sometimes survived in folklore, for example on the Isle of Man where the mountain Slieau Whallian is said to be the place where witches were punished by being rolled down the hillside in spiked barrels. This was only the final stage of the procedure, for the suspected witch was first thrown into the Curragh Glass, a swamp at the foot of the mountain. If she drowned, she was considered innocent of witchcraft and given a Christian burial; but if she managed to drag herself out of the swamp alive, she was declared guilty of witchcraft and either burned alive or rolled downhill in the spiked barrel. No wonder it is believed that on stormy nights the voice of a murdered witch can be heard through the howling wind on Slieau Whallian. Knock Hill near Crieff (Perth) was also the site of a witch murder, the victim being named as Catharine Niven who lived in a cave on the hill until she was dragged out, strangled and burned. Not far away at Dunning there is a memorial to witch murder: a cross on a pile of stones, with the written inscription, 'Maggie Wall burnt here 1657 as a Witch' (*see plate 4*).

Hills were often used as places of execution, and gibbets set up, and in at least one instance a hill's name commemorates an execution there – or maybe we should say allegedly commemorates an execution, for there is no certainty that the story is true: it may have been invented to explain the hill's unusual name. The hill in question is called Robin-a-Tiptoe, Leicestershire's second highest hill near Tilton, and it is said that in 1586 a very tall man was hanged there. But his toes brushed the ground as he hung on the gibbet, and when he was cut down he was found to be still alive, and he escaped with his life. Men were also executed on another Leicestershire hill, Croft Hill, where in December 1124 the local overlord had forty-four men killed after accusing them of theft. It is said that weeping and moaning can be heard on the hill on December nights.

If we cannot be sure about the reality of tales of witchcraft, murder and execution, we know that we are safely in the realms of fantasy when we write about dragons roaming the British countryside. Whole books have been written about British dragons, many places with dragon legends can be visited, and carvings of dragons can be seen in many British churches. Dragons will also appear in other chapters in this book, but here we will describe some hills where they were said to live. Dragons often took the form of gigantic serpents with long tails, which they liked to coil around a hill, such as Linton Hill (Roxburgh) which was also known as Wormiston, and appears to have marks on it left by the dragon's coils. The hill can be seen from Linton church, and a worn carving over the south door of the church shows a knight and two monsters, one of which he is attacking with a lance. This is said to show the dragon being slain. Similarly in Durham the so-called Lambton Worm ('worm' being another name for a dragon) liked to coil itself around Worm Hill at Lambton Castle near Chester-le-Street, its tail stretching ten times round the hill, and again leaving marks. It was eventually killed by the Knight of Lambton. In Oxfordshire the site of a dragon-slaying can still be seen, marked by a bare patch where the dragon's blood fell. This is on Dragon Hill* at Uffington, just below the great Uffington White Horse (or dragon) cut out of the chalk hillside. The dragon was slain by St George on top of the conical chalk hill, and where its poisonous blood soaked into the ground, no grass will grow to this day. It is also said that the dragon lies buried in the hill. The dragon which terrorized Bisterne (Hampshire) lived on nearby Burley Beacon, from where it descended every day to drink a pail of milk which the villagers had to supply. A knight was hired to fight this foe, and to protect himself against its poisonous breath he covered his body with birdlime and powdered glass. He managed to slay the beast, but died himself soon afterwards.

We described earlier how many hills and mountains were brought into being by the magical exploits of the Devil, or giants, or hero figures. These characters were also said to use the hills for pastimes such as fighting battles or, in the Devil's case, playing quoits, which he did with King Arthur on Blackingstone and Hel Tor on Dartmoor (Devon). The match was not entirely amicable, each standing on a hill and hurling quoits back and forth. King Arthur won, but the Devil did not take his defeat gracefully. He turned the quoits to stone, and they are today the rocks that crown each of the two tors. In the Clwydian Hills (Clwyd), King Arthur had a battle with the giant Benlli Gawr on Cefn y Gadfa (The Ridge of the Battle), and he also fought the giant Rhita on Snowdon (Gwynedd). Rhita lived on the mountain, and had a cloak made out of the beards of kings he had killed. He wanted Arthur's beard and so challenged him to single combat on the mountain, the winner taking both the cloak and the loser's beard. Arthur was victorious and won the cloak; Rhita was buried on Snowdon's summit and stones placed over his body, the resulting cairn being known in the nineteenth century as Carnedd y Gawr (The Giant's Cairn), but it is no longer in existence. Jack o' Legs was a Hertfordshire giant who used to rob the rich to feed the poor, until he was caught and hanged. (His grave can still be seen in Weston churchyard, 14 feet long.) When he was practising his form of philanthropy, Jack's Hill north of Graveley was where he had his look-out, watching for rich travellers to rob.

The fame of some folk heroes has spread throughout Britain, such as King Arthur whose name is linked to a great many natural landscape features with legends to explain his presence there. Others like Jack o' Legs have a much more local fame. Owain Glyndwr (Owen Glendower) was a Welsh hero who lived from *c*.1354 to *c*.1416. He was the leader of the Welsh people in their fight against English dominance, and he disappeared when the Welsh uprising against the English was finally suppressed, though some believed that he was in hiding somewhere and would emerge to lead his people when the time was right. One of his homes when alive was at Carrog near Corwen (Clwyd), and there was a story that Glyndwr was seen nearby in the Berwyn Mountains by the Abbot of Valle Crucis Abbey. The tall figure emerging from the mist said, 'Good morning, Sir Abbot, you have got up early this morning.' Recognizing Owain Glyndwr, the Abbot replied: 'No my Lord, it is you who have risen too early – a hundred years too early.' He was referring, of course, to the prophecy that Glyndwr would reappear when needed by his people. The hero nodded 'Yes' and disappeared back into the mist, never to be seen again.

Ghosts aplenty roam the hills and mountains, from horses and giants to a whole phantom army. The horse was a white one, seen in 1971 by a couple driving on Leesthorpe Hill near Burton Lazars, Leicestershire. It leapt across the road in front of them, leaving them shaken and puzzled. They later discovered that it had been seen by others from time to time, and a local story told how the horse had belonged to a chieftain, but had been slain by him after his son fell from the horse and died. He immediately regretted his action, and saw the horse's reappearance in ghost form as a reproach to him for killing it. In Devon a phantom sow has been seen, with piglets, on Merripit Hill, Dartmoor. They are hungry, and are making for Cator Gate near Widecombe where, so they have heard, food is waiting in the form of a dead horse. But when they arrive it has been eaten, and, so thin are they as they wander slowly back, they dissolve into the mist and disappear. Another pig ghost was in fact the Devil in disguise. A man called John Roberts, walking over Aberdare mountain (Mid Glamorgan), met a handsome man wearing a cocked hat, red waistcoat and blue coat, who asked the way to Aberdare. As Roberts looked at him, he saw a cloven hoof and a long tail beneath the blue coat, and realized who the stranger was. The Devil then changed into a pig, grunted, and ran away.

On the Black Mountain (south-west Herefordshire, on the border with Gwent and Powys) the Devil took the form of a large black crow which would extinguish travellers' lights so that they lost their way. But one traveller on the Black Mountain had the opposite experience when walking from Llanthony to Longtown. He lost his way in the fog and was standing wondering which way to go when a man came towards him. He wore a cloak and a large broad-brimmed hat and didn't speak, but simply beckoned; the lost man followed, and found himself on the right path again. His rescuer vanished into the fog. When he later described him to his friends, they told him he had seen a local man who knew the mountain well – but who had been dead for two years. Not very far away, in Cwm Clydach near Brynmawr (Gwent) another man had a very different experience when returning home from his work over the mountain. He saw a light ahead of him, apparently from a lantern carried by another man, and thinking it was a workmate also going home, he increased his speed in order to catch him up and have the benefit of the lamp when going down the steep, rocky path. The rather short man seemed to be moving very quickly for his size, but the traveller continued to hurry after him – until suddenly he found himself on the brink of a precipice, and within a stone's throw of plunging into the roaring river in the gorge below. The little man with the lantern sprang lightly across the gap to the opposite side, turned and laughed before snuffing out his light and disappearing up the hill. He was a Pwcca, one of the fairy family, and the place where this encounter took place was known as Cwm Pwcca, or the Pwcca's Valley.

In Scotland, climbers on Ben Macdhui, a 4,000-foot mountain in the Cairngorms (Aberdeen), have sometimes encountered the Big Grey Man. The classic occasion was in 1891 when Professor Norman Collie was alone on the mountain. Describing his experience thirty-four years later, he said:

'I was returning from the cairn on the summit in a mist when I began to think I heard something else than merely the noise of my own footsteps. For every few steps I took I heard a crunch, and then another crunch as if someone was walking after me but taking steps three or four times the length of my own. I said to myself, "This is all nonsense." I listened and heard it again, but could see nothing in the mist. As I walked on and the eerie crunch, crunch, sounded behind me I was seized with terror and took to my heels, staggering blindly among the boulders for four or five miles down to Rothiemurchus Forest. Whatever you make of it I do not know, but there is something very queer about the top of Ben Macdhui and I will not go back there again by myself I know.'

After Professor Collie had reported his experience, another climber on the mountain, Dr A.M. Kellas who had also climbed on Mount Everest, told how he had actually seen the Big Grey

Man, one day when he and his brother had been just below the summit of Ben Macdhui. On seeing the giant figure coming towards them, they fled. It has been suggested that the figure they saw was similar to the 'Brocken Spectre', a phenomenon first seen on the Brocken in Germany's Harz Mountains, when the observer's shadow is thrown against a wall of mist. But it is unlikely that three such experienced climbers would have mistaken natural sounds or shadows for a giant figure, and other people claim to have encountered him too, as well as hearing unearthly music, and voices talking, laughing and chanting.

A similar phenomenon has been experienced on Boar of Badenoch, a hill above the Drumochter Pass (Inverness), when two men out hunting earlier this century saw two huge figures moving quickly along a streak of mist at the skyline above them, then stopping as if looking down at the two men. They seemed to be only 100 yards away, and one of the witnesses said, 'It was an extraordinary experience seeing those great figures out there on the hillside. It was certainly uncanny and I felt myself shiver although that day was not unduly cold.' As they watched, the two figures disappeared as if climbing out of sight. Were they shadows cast by the sun onto the mist? A similar phenomenon would seem to have been experienced in the mountains of Wales in past ages. The figure was called the Brenin Llwyd or Grey King, and he was said to sit among the mountains clad in clouds and mist. Children were warned not to wander into the mountains, or else he would catch them.

A great misty figure, but this time female, was said to haunt Bicknoller Hill (Somerset), where she herded red deer. The Old Woman of the Mountain haunts Llanhilleth Mountain (Gwent), crying 'Wow up!' (an anglicized version of the Welsh 'Wwb!', a cry of distress), and sometimes the cry was heard though the Old Woman was not seen. Anyone who did see her would lose their way, even though they might be perfectly familiar with the area. Seeing her ahead of them, they would hurry after her, calling for her to wait, but they would not be able to catch her, however fast they ran, and she was likely to lead them into a bog, with an evil sense of humour like that of the Pwcca we met earlier.

Other strange hill-top hauntings include what appeared to be a flock of sheep on Cefen Rhychdir, Bedwellty (Gwent) which vanished into thin air, only to reappear later but seen as different things by different people – greyhounds, pigs, naked children – as if rising out of the earth. These events were seen 'in the shade of the mountain between them [the witnesses] and the sun': another Brocken Spectre type of natural phenomenon? It was the Devil who was responsible for the haunting and taunting and finally the death of a young man in Lancashire. He was crossing Fair Snape Fell at night when he came to a place said to be haunted by the Devil. But he didn't see the usual devilish figure: instead he saw a beautiful girl with long golden hair. Entranced, he went over to her, but she vanished when he was a few feet away. He returned to the spot night after night, neglecting the girl to whom he was engaged, and eventually confessing to the angry girl what he was up to. But he refused to stop visiting his ghostly love, and became so ill that he had to be put to bed in a delirium. He got up before he was fully recovered and crept out of the house on a misty night. He was found on the Fell the next morning, lying dead with an expression of horror on his face. Beside him in the soft soil were the imprints of cloven hooves. It must also have been the Devil who haunted Creech Hill near Bruton (Somerset), causing terror to anyone who encountered him. A farmer going home from market saw something lying in the road and went to help the person he supposed to be lying there. But as he approached, the figure rose up to a great height and screamed, sending the farmer running away, with the creature following him until he collapsed at his home. Another man who had to cross the hill late at night took a stout stick, and used it when something tall and black rose out of the ground before him. But the stick went through the phantom, and the man found that he could not move, as if his feet were stuck to the ground. Evil laughter echoed around him, and he had to stay there until the first light of dawn.

Phantom armies have sometimes been seen, as for example on Grange Hill (Dorset) where in 1678 Captain John Lawrence and about a hundred other people saw what looked like an army of thousands marching with much noise and clashing of weapons. The alarm was raised in Wareham, but by the time preparations had been made to counter this unknown enemy, they had vanished. Phantom horsemen, though only twelve of them, were seen in 1956 on Hunters Tor, Lustleigh Cleave (Devon). The riders wore medieval costume and their horses were brightly decorated. The two witnesses followed on their own horses, until the group were hidden by a stone wall. When the witnesses passed this, the other riders had vanished, and an hour's search revealed no trace of them. The only hoof-prints in the soft ground were the ones their own horses had made. But the most famous phantom army must be the one that appeared on Souther Fell (Cumbria) in 1735. It took an hour for the marching army to pass the witness, and no one believed him when he reported what he had seen, but two years later, on the same day of the year, Midsummer Eve, the master of the first witness also saw the phantom army in the same place. They were seen again a few years later, so that about twenty-six people saw them in total, but whatever it was is unlikely to have been a real army, because the ground was very rocky and the number of marching men so vast. Was it another optical illusion?

It is unlikely that the phantom black dogs seen in so many locations throughout Britain are optical illusions, though eliminating one possible explanation takes us no nearer to deciding what the answer to this mystery really is. So many people have reported meeting black dogs – which are usually calf-sized, often with fiery red eyes, and clearly not 'real' dogs – that the phenomenon must be taken seriously. These dogs also exist in folklore, and with older accounts it is not always possible to tell whether a tale is true or merely legendary. Hills where black dogs have been seen include Meon Hill (Warwickshire) where a dog was seen on nine successive evenings by Charles Walton, a ploughboy who was later murdered on the hill, as recounted earlier. On the ninth occasion, a headless woman in a silk gown ran past him, and he then heard that his sister had died. In the Somerset Quantocks, a man was guided home by a black dog after he got lost on top of Weacombe in a sea mist. He thought the dog was his own sheepdog, but when they arrived home he saw the dog grow first larger, then fade away. Winsford Hill in Somerset also has its black dog, which stops travellers. He must stand still while it slowly disappears until only its large glowing eyes are visible; if he moves closer, he will soon die. The black dog of Birdlip Hill (Gloucestershire) helps lost travellers, like the dog in the Quantocks. In Shropshire, Edric Wild (also called Wild Edric and Edric the Wild) was an eleventh-century landowner who led a resistance against the incoming Normans and so became a folk hero. It was said that he was seen riding over the hills just before the outbreak of the Crimean War, and his ghost was said to haunt the Stretton Hills in the form of a black dog with fiery eyes.

Packs of ghostly dogs, known as the Wild Hunt, Yeth Hounds, in Wales as the Cwn Annwn, and various other local names, were believed to haunt many hills and mountains throughout Britain, such as the Berwyns (Clwyd), where a girl who found herself among them only saved herself by repeating the Lord's Prayer over and over again until the dogs ran away; Radnor Forest, Kerry Hills and Plynlimon (all in Powys), the dogs having their kennels in the last; Ditchling Beacon (Sussex); the Quantock Hills (Somerset); Dartmoor (Devon); and many other places. They came from the spirit world, and their howling was believed to be an omen of death. Descriptions of them vary widely, and they seem to appear in all colours – black, white as snow, spotted red, with glittering eyes and tiny rose-coloured ears, dripping blood, and so on. Sometimes the packs travel alone, sometimes with a master, who may ride on horseback. In Wales he was Arawn, King of the Underworld; in Worcestershire he was Harry-ca-Nab who hunted across the Lickey Hills on stormy nights, mounted on a winged horse or wild bull; in other places he was the Devil himself. There are innumerable stories of human encounters with the Wild Hunt, usually preceding a death, and it was naturally advisable to avoid meeting or seeing them.

Rivers and Streams

In contrast to the previous chapter, not much of the folklore of watercourses has to do with how a river or stream was formed. Instead, most of the lore concerns beings of some kind: gods, spirits, ghosts, the Devil, witches, mermaids, fairies, monsters . . . and underlying this is the belief that the rivers themselves are living entities. On the mountain Plynlimon (Dyfed/Powys), for example, can be found the sources of three major rivers, the Severn, Wye and Rheidol, and it was said that the three emerged simultaneously and ran a race to the sea. The Rheidol reached the sea three weeks before her bigger 'sisters' – they were seen as female beings.

Before we consider the personification of rivers in more detail and tell of the beings that haunt them, here are a few tales which do relate to the form and appearance of watercourses. The Constable Sands, sandbanks at the mouth of the River Dee (Cheshire), were said to have been miraculously formed by St Werburgh in answer to a prayer. The Constable of Chester was the supplicant: he was trying to help Earl Richard who had gone on a pilgrimage to St Winefride's Well* at Holywell (Clwyd) across the far side of the wide Dee estuary. The hostility of the Welsh meant that he had had to take refuge in Basingwerke Abbey and the Constable was trying to get across the Dee to help him, but was unable to do so until the sandbanks suddenly appeared, following his prayer to the saint. St Tydecho was another holy man who featured in a watercourse legend, the one which explained the whiteness of a stream, the Llaethnant (Milk Stream) near Llanymawddwy (Gwynedd). He lived at this place, and his milking fold was in the hills above the village. A milk-maid slipped and spilt the milk she was carrying into the stream while trying to cross it at a ford near the milking fold. St Tydecho wasn't angry with her: instead he converted the whole stream to milk for the benefit of the poor people. It is easy to see why this mountain stream should have reminded people of milk, for it forms numerous small waterfalls as it makes its way out of the hills and the water appears white every time it froths over the rocks. Reddish water in a stream trickling down Blackgang Chine on the Isle of Wight was said to be blood, after a curse was placed on the Giant of Chale who lived there. An island saint confronted the giant, whose favourite meal was human flesh, and cursed him, whereupon the ogre and his monsters disappeared, leaving only the bloody water behind.

There is a river in Cumbria which flows through large swallow holes (holes in limestone rock where the water passes underground for a short distance), and when the river is high, one of these holes appears to be full of boiling water, which is why it is known as the Fairies' Kettle. Here the river appears to boil: further north, the River Shin (Sutherland) is said never to freeze. This came about, so the legend goes, because Christ used to visit the remote Highland rivers, especially during the winter when there was no one about, and he would watch the birds and animals and fishes. One frosty night when he was at the River Shin, he saw that the fish appeared troubled, and he enquired of a large salmon what was the matter. It told him that they feared the cold weather when the river would freeze; whereupon Christ blessed the river and said that the salmon need not fear because the river would never freeze again.

Some rivers were believed to conceal hidden treasure, for example the Ogmore in Mid Glamorgan. It was said that people with money or precious stones would never rest if their wealth remained hidden after their death, and in order that the spirit should be at rest the treasure must be taken and thrown into the river by a living person. But not against the flow of the current, or else that person would be tormented for ever. Numerous detailed folk stories were told which illustrated this strange belief that treasure had to be thrown into the River Ogmore. In Northumberland, there was a legend that treasure was hidden in the depths of a pool in the River Allen. A treasure seeker who used two horses and two oxen to pull it out, shouted as the treasure appeared: 'Hup, Brock! Hup, Bran! We'll have it out in spite of god or man!' Whereupon the treasure, together with the horses and oxen, all disappeared back into the pool. It was said that in fine weather you could see the oxen's horns where they stood upright on the river bed. Lost church bells are sometimes said to lie inaccessibly on riverbeds, and in the case of Marden church bell (Herefordshire) it was held there by a mermaid after it fell in by accident. A wise man told the people how to overcome the mermaid and retrieve the bell, but stressed that the procedure must be carried out in silence. They succeeded in pulling the bell to the surface, with the mermaid asleep inside it, but one of the workmen cried out: 'In spite of all the devils in hell, now we'll land Marden's great bell!' At which the mermaid awoke and took the bell back into the water, where it still lies, sometimes ringing in answer to the church bells. A silver bell said to be somewhere in the water at the bottom of the waterfall in St Nectan's Glen* (Cornwall) was thrown there by St Nectan, who was buried under the waterfall along with his treasure. Some miners who tried to find the treasure heard a bell ringing and a voice saying: 'The child is not yet born who shall recover this treasure.'

So far, the rivers we have described have been neutral towards humans, even benevolent in some cases, but this is unusual for, where a river or stream features in folklore, it is usually represented in a way that is threatening to humans. The commonest form this takes is the belief that the river periodically demands a human sacrifice, a belief which attaches to many of the major rivers of Britain. The River Don (South Yorkshire) was said to claim a child each year, possibly a memory of child sacrifice in past ages; while the River Parrett (Somerset) was believed to take one life annually, a man, woman and child in turn. The River Dart on Dartmoor (Devon) also demands an annual sacrifice, the noise it sometimes makes while rushing round the Broad Stone being interpreted as a voice calling for its due, as in the saying:

> *Dart, Dart, cruel Dart,*
> *Every year thou claim'st a heart.*

It was said that one year a farm lad believed he was the river's next victim. One night, he shouted 'Dart's calling me!' and ran off into the darkness, never to be seen again. In her book *The Witchcraft and Folklore of Dartmoor,* Ruth St Leger-Gordon wrote that a native of Dartmoor had told her how one day he had seen a farmer he knew standing on the edge of the fast-flowing East Okement River. He sensed that the man was about to jump in, so he hurried down to him. As he did so, he clearly heard the river say, 'The hour has come, but not the man', as if a sacrifice was due, but the wrong person had presented himself. This phrase is not unique to this event, and will be met with again in Chapter 6 where we explore the folklore of pools and lakes.

Many other rivers also claim victims: the Eager, a tidal-wave on the River Trent (recalling Aegir, the god of the ocean in Norse mythology, once worshipped in northern England), called for three lives a year, the Scottish Dee also needs three (though the Cheshire Dee takes none), and Scottish rivers Tweed, Till and Spey also demand lives. In Lancashire it was the spirit of the River Ribble, called Peg o' Nell, who needed a life every seven years, unless she was appeased with the sacrifice of a cockerel or an animal instead. It has been suggested that the idea of spirits living in rivers and demanding sacrifices is a memory of the Celtic worship of river gods and goddesses and of the rituals that were performed. Alternatively the tales of frightful hags living in the rivers might sometimes have simply been invented by mothers to keep their children from straying too close to the water. A Gwent river spirit was called Nicky Nicky Nye, and children were told how he lived in fast-flowing streams and in pools of stagnant water, waiting to grab children who got too close. One girl was nearly taken by him when she was playing by the River Usk: a gnarled hand came out of the water and made a grab at her clothes. It was said of the River Severn (Shropshire) that anyone who had caused death by drowning in that river should never try to cross the river in a boat, for long arms would reach out and pull him under the water.

People who had been drowned could be located in different ways in different rivers. In the River Wye (Herefordshire), for example, a loaf containing quicksilver should be thrown into the river, and it would stop where the body could be found. Also, the body would float on the ninth day. Any Christian who drowned in the River Dee (Cheshire) could be recovered for Christian burial because a light would shine over the place where the body could be found. At Llanilar (Dyfed) the drowning of a woman in the River Ystwyth was predicted by the shining of a corpse candle (a pale hovering light which foretold a death) over the river a short time beforehand.

To return to the theme of river spirits: these often (though not invariably) seem to have been women, and so old tales of women haunting rivers may be vague memories of river goddesses. One such was Peg Powler, the spirit of the River Tees (Durham), who was said to lie in wait for people who got too close to the river, and then drag them under the water to drown. Children were warned to beware of her: they would recognise her by her long green hair. Froth seen floating on the river was called 'Peg Powler's suds', and a finer kind of foam was known as 'Peg Powler's cream'. An equally ugly hag who haunted the stream called Nant-y-Gledyr and the swamp through which it flowed at Caerphilly (Mid Glamorgan) was known as the Gwrach-y-rhibyn. She had bat-like wings, long black hair, and fingers like talons, and she would emerge from the water, wring her hands, and moan or groan, then fly over to Caerphilly Castle where she would hide (*see plate 5*). She was also seen at other South Wales rivers, such as the Thaw near Cowbridge (South Glamorgan), and in some ways she resembled the Irish banshee. A scowling woman dressed in green haunted the River Conon (Ross and Cromarty), leaping out of the water and beckoning to passers-by to follow her, which would inevitably be a fatal course of action. One man clung to a tree when she appeared, but she still dragged him to his death in the river.

A woman in a small boat was said to haunt the River Wye at Hereford. It was believed that every evening at eight she would set sail for about 3 miles to a village called Northbrigg (no longer in existence) where she would land on the bank, crying and moaning, then shortly re-embark and sail back to Hereford. Why she did this, no one knew. Of the girl who was said to haunt the River Goyt at Marple (Cheshire), it was explained that her lover had drowned in the river. There are many other tales and legends of women haunting rivers and streams, often because this was where a lover died. These 'women in white', for they usually are so clad, may be nothing more than wisps of mist, seen as ghosts by nervous passers-by and then given a kind of life by being woven into a tale of love and death. Or they may indeed some-times represent the last surviving memories of the river goddesses worshipped by our pagan ancestors.

Very occasionally the ghostly figure haunting a stretch of water is male, as in Dyfed where the Pool of the Harper in the River Teifi near Llandyssul was haunted by a harper who had been drowned there long ago. From time to time the sound of a harp could be heard, as the spirit made music in the pool. The stream below the waterfall in Glen Maye (Isle of Man) was believed to be haunted by a man who had been drowned after getting on the back of an animal he thought was a horse, but which was in fact a tarroo ushtey, the equivalent of the Scottish kelpie (of which more later), and which ran into the sea with him. A little man wearing a cap and holding a fishing rod was seen sitting on the banks of the River Rivelin near Sheffield (South Yorkshire): he disappeared when the witness approached him. Being described as a small man, was this indeed one of the Little

People, the fairies? They are known to frequent rivers and streams, as shown by place names such as the Fairy Glen on the River Conwy near Betws-y-Coed (Gwynedd) where they were said to play. Other watery locations where folklore has placed them include the River Neath in West Glamorgan and Cottingley Beck in West Yorkshire. In the latter case they were allegedly seen in the early years of this century by two girls who were inspired by their encounters to fabricate photographs of traditional fairies with gossamer wings, to 'prove' that they really had seen them. The photographs were so convincing that it was to be many decades before the hoax was finally revealed.

From human-like ghosts and spirits haunting watercourses to some rather more inhuman beings: a ragbag of tales, in fact, whose only link is that they are all associated with rivers or streams. The River Trent was believed to be haunted by a pygmy-like being with the face of a seal and long hair, which would cross the river in a small boat looking like a pie-dish, using tiny oars no bigger than teaspoons. This was at a bend known as Jenny Hurn, between Wildsworth and Owston Ferry (South Humberside/Lincolnshire border). The presence of this 'boggard' made boatmen loth to anchor on the bend at night, and they claimed to know by instinct when it was about. The Black Rock in the estuary of the River Mersey (Merseyside), on the other hand, was believed to be haunted by a beautiful mermaid. According to the story in an eighteenth-century chap-book, she appeared to a sailor named John Robinson, who persuaded her to come aboard his vessel, where he kept her for a while. She gave him a ring before returning to the water, but future happiness was not to be his, either with or without his mermaid lover, because he died five days afterwards, in the 'safety' of his own home. We will meet more mermaids later, in Chapter 5 on cliffs and coasts, and in Chapter 6 on pools and lakes, for there have been several others supposedly seen around Britain.

Two groups of white-robed ladies were seen crossing the River Towy near Carmarthen (Dyfed) on more than one occasion by a young man who was curious about their activities, as they were so secretive and seemed to disappear on reaching the far shore. He hid and watched, and was rewarded when moonlight shone on them as they reached the middle of the river. He saw that they were sailing in cockle-shells, and when they reached the bank the ladies disappeared and he could see only black cats. He had been watching the white witches of Carmarthen. Witches are not commonly associated with water, and neither are giants. But the Clwyd giant Benlli was finally outwitted by a river, the Alun west of Mold, in the foothills of the Clwydian Hills. Benlli's stronghold was Foel Fenlli, a hill in the Clwydian range, and he was finally despatched by St Cynhafal. When the saint climbed the hill to talk to him, Benlli lobbed boulders in his direction, and the saint suggested he learn to control his temper. But Benlli kept on with his attack, so St Cynhafal put his hands together and prayed, whereupon Benlli's temper flared up, literally, and he burst into flames. He shot off the hill and down into the River Alun, hoping to dowse the fire in its water, but the river refused to help and flowed down a hole, leaving the giant high and dry. He tried again a mile or so downstream, but again the river flowed into a hole, and the giant was finally consumed, leaving only a pile of ashes. Ever since that time, the river every summer disappears into two swallow holes.

Llyn-y-Geulan-Goch is a pool in the River Dee near Llanfor, a village close to Bala (Gwynedd), and it was here that an evil spirit was imprisoned. The spirit would appear inside Llanfor church as a gentleman wearing a cocked hat, he would light up the church at night, and he would cause poltergeist-type phenomena, but he never harmed anyone. Nevertheless he was a nuisance, so it was decided to remove him, and two gentlemen skilled in divination were brought to the church. They spoke to him and told him they intended to take him to his rest, and after a struggle they removed him from the church. He was in the shape of a cockerel at this point, and they took him on horseback to the river, crossing the two fields between church and river in two leaps. The evil spirit had no desire to be imprisoned in the water and fought against his captors, nearly succeeding in taking them with him, but he finally agreed to go if they would lie face down while he jumped in. They did so, and heard a splash. The spirit has to stay in the pool until he has counted all the sand in it. There are in fact several other versions of the story of how the evil spirit was ejected from Llanfor church and imprisoned in the river. Such a punishment for evil-doing is often met with in folklore, and another story tells how Sir John Wynne is imprisoned beneath the Swallow Falls near Betws-y-Coed (Gwynedd). He can be heard struggling with his fetters and making hideous cries as the waterfall cascades over him.

The spirits dwelling in rivers and streams sometimes take animal form, though the animals are often monstrous, or capable of shape-shifting. The creature encountered most often is the kelpie, a Scottish water-horse, haunting rivers rather than lochs or the sea. It could also appear as a shaggy man, jumping up behind a lone horse-rider and frightening him out of his wits. His other trick was to appear as a horse and persuade people on to his back, whereupon he would rush into the river and they would be drowned. This may be another variant of the theme that rivers demand human sacrifices, as is strongly suggested by a tale about the kelpie of the River Conon (Ross and Cromarty), which appeared at midday and cried out, 'Behold the hour has come, but not the man' three times, then disappeared into a pool. Soon the farm workers who had witnessed this saw a man riding towards the river, and so they went to intercept him, to warn him not to go near the water. But he laughed at them and would have taken no notice, so they had to hang on to his horse's bridle and even kidnap him and shut him in an old church nearby. Once one o'clock had struck they felt that he would now be safe, but when they opened the church door to release him, he wasn't there. They eventually found him – drowned in a couple of inches of water in an old stone trough.

Among the numerous other Scottish rivers that were believed to harbour kelpies was the Spey (Moray/Banff/Inverness), where a beautiful white horse would walk beside weary travellers until they became so tired that they climbed on its back, at which it would gallop off at breakneck speed and plunge into one of the river's deep pools, the rider being unable to jump free. On stormy nights the horse's whinnying could be heard, so it was said. The kelpie of the Strichen Burn (Aberdeen) could assume human form and speak in a human voice, and a traveller who heard someone addressing him looked round and saw an old man darning a pair of trousers. For some unknown reason, he struck the old man, who promptly turned into a horse and disappeared into the river. The kelpie of the River Don (Aberdeen) once appeared in human form, offering to carry across the flooded river a man who was anxious to reach a relative's deathbed. He agreed, but when they reached the middle of the river the kelpie turned into a horse and tried to take the traveller down into the river. Unusually, he managed to escape and scrambled to the riverbank, whereupon the thwarted kelpie threw a large boulder after him which still sits on the bank and is known as the Kelpie's Stane.

Although he is primarily a Scottish beast, the water-horse also appears in the folklore of other areas of Britain, especially Wales. There was a Ceffyl-dwr (water-horse in Welsh) which haunted the banks of the River Towy around Carmarthen (Dyfed), and one man who went down the river in a coracle returned on the back of the Ceffyl-dwr, which had eyes like balls of fire. In North Wales the water-horses were said to associate with the mountain ponies, and the small horses known as merlyns were direct descendants of the Ceffyl-dwr. In various parts of Wales, the water-horse could take varying forms: a goat, a frog, a squirrel, for example, and it would leap onto people's backs. Near Glyn-Neath (West Glamorgan) it was said to have appeared out of the river as a snow-white horse, and as in Scotland it had tempted a weary traveller to climb on to its back. But instead of taking him into the river to drown, it travelled at great speed over hill and dale, appearing not to touch the ground, until at last he was thrown off its back. When he recovered he looked around and saw the horse become indistinct as it gradually merged into a cloud hanging over the hill. The man made his way down the hill and found that he was at Llanddewi Brefi (Dyfed), some 35 miles (as the crow flies) from his starting point. The journey had taken about an hour.

In England water-horses are much rarer. One of the few was

said to live in the River Wharfe south of Barden Bridge (North Yorkshire), at a place called the Strid where the river runs fast in a narrow channel. It was believed to come out of the river on May Day, along with a fairy who would grant people's wishes, and predict the future. But three sisters who wanted to take advantage of this were later found drowned: just as with the kelpie's deceptive offer of help, a trick was used to lure people to the water.

Other monsters live in the rivers and streams, though closer investigation may sometimes reveal a down-to-earth explanation for the legend, as in the case of the buggane or evil spirit which was said to inhabit a waterfall in Maughold parish (Isle of Man). This buggane would often be heard wailing and screaming, but a Manxman with a scientific mind discovered that the noises were only heard when the wind was in a certain direction, and he concluded that they were caused by the wind blowing through a narrow cleft in the rock below the fall. The Scottish Shellycoat, a water-dwelling spirit, was not so easily disposed of. He wore a coat made of shells which clattered when he moved. One of the rivers he haunted was Ettrick Water (Selkirk), where he played a trick on two men who were by the river bank on one dark night. They heard a voice crying 'Lost! Lost!', and thought it was someone on the point of drowning, so they went in its direction. It seemed to be moving along the river, and they followed it throughout the stormy night until they reached the source of the river. They were amazed to hear the voice moving up the mountainside, and wearily gave up their quest, at which they heard Shellycoat laughing at having deceived them so successfully.

In contrast, a North Wales legend tells how a water monster was defeated by human ingenuity. The creature was the afanc that lived in the Afanc's Pool in the River Conwy near Betws-y-Coed (Gwynedd), from where it would venture out into the surrounding countryside and steal cattle and in other ways make a nuisance of itself. No one was able to kill it, for their weapons made no impression on it, so it was decided to try and remove it to somewhere where it would cause less trouble. A young girl enticed it from the pool, and it went to sleep with its head resting

34

on her knee and its hand on her breast. While it was sleeping, the men fastened chains around it. On waking and seeing the chains, it went back into the pool, taking the girl's breast with it, but a long chain was held by the men, and using oxen they were able to haul the afanc from the river and drag it for 10 miles or more over the mountains, finally dumping it in the lake now known as Glaslyn, below Snowdon's summit. Various markers along the route acquired names which commemorate the epic journey: a pass was called Bwlch Rhiw'r Ychen (pass of the slope of the oxen); the place where one of the oxen lost an eye was called the Moor of the Ox's Eye, and later when it became a pool, the Pool of the Ox's Eye.

Dragons, serpents and worms also favoured rivers and streams. A monstrous serpent was believed to live in a bottomless whirlpool in the River Taff at Cardiff (South Glamorgan), and it would eat the bodies of people who had drowned in the river and been sucked into the whirlpool, which was why their bodies were often not found. But if a drowned body was recovered, it was believed that that person must have been very good, because the serpent would not touch righteous people. It was also said that a beautiful woman lured young men into the whirlpool to their deaths: she was the Devil in disguise. Also in South Wales, the flying serpent of Newcastle Emlyn (Dyfed) in the Teifi valley was enticed to its death in the river. It had a hard shell covering its body, except the navel, and so a soldier stood in the river and shot at it as it rested on the castle, aiming for the navel. He then laid a red flannel on the water and swam for the shore. The serpent came down and attacked the red flannel, but it had been mortally wounded, and the river flowed red with its blood. Another winged serpent made its lair in the rocks near the top of a famous North Wales waterfall, Pistyll Rhaeadr near Llanrhaeadr-ym-Mochnant on the Powys/Clwyd border (*see plate 9*). Y Gwiber (the Viper) would cool itself in the water flowing over the falls, and they would sometimes be tinged red with the blood of its prey. Many attempts were made to kill it, including dropping huge boulders down on it from the top of the falls, but no one succeeded until a local wise woman told them what to do. They dragged a tall stone out into a field, covered it with sharp spikes, and draped a red cloth over it. As night fell they lit a fire to attract the Gwiber, which came over to investigate and, seeing the cloth-covered pillar, it attacked with its full strength, perhaps mistaking it for an enemy. But as it attacked, so the spikes drove into its body, until it finally fell dead from loss of blood. The stone can still be seen: a standing stone near the village, called Post Coch (Red Pillar) or Post-y-Wiber (Pillar of the Serpent).

The Lambton Worm, which we have already met in Chapter 1, also lived in a river, in this case the River Wear in Durham, until it was caught by the heir of Lambton when he was fishing (it was at this stage only a small worm, though ugly) and thrown into a nearby well, where it grew apace. When it outgrew the well, it crept back into the river where it lay coiled round a rock during the day, at night twining nine times round the nearby Worm Hill. It was by this time about 2 miles long, with an appetite to match, and steps had to be taken to get rid of it. The heir to Lambton consulted a wise woman, and on her advice made himself a coat of chain-mail studded with razor-sharp blades. Dressed in this, he stood on a crag in the river, where he was found by the worm who wound himself around the knight. The worm cut his own body into pieces as he did so. The parts fell into the river and were washed away, so that they could not magically reunite, and in this way was the Lambton Worm defeated.

Caves and Hollows

Giants make them, fairies live in them, musicians get lost in them, heroes sleep in them . . . Caves are put to numerous uses in folklore; and hollows, gorges, crevices, and assorted holes also feature in similar kinds of tales. To begin at the beginning, with the ways in which they are made, we find two giants, brothers Bronwen and Idris who were active in the Welsh mountains, building towers on mountain tops many miles apart, from which they intended to shout to each other. They only had one hammer, which they shared, throwing it back and forth across the landscape. Bronwen seemed to be using the hammer more than his fair share of the time, and so his tower was growing faster. His brother lost his temper when Bronwen called for the hammer yet again, and threw it with all his might, so that it flew over Bronwen who was on the Berwyn Mountains and landed at Cwm Llawenog in Llanarmon Dyffryn Ceiriog (Clwyd), leaving a dent in the ground now called Pant-y-Cawr or the Giant's Hollow. In Durham, a hammer was shared by three giants and when a blind giant threw the hammer it fell short and made a hollow dene called Howden, near Consett. Back in Clwyd,

37

hollows in fields at Tan-y-Gaer farm, Llannefydd, are called Naid y Cawr a'r Gawres, or the Leap of the Giant and Giantess because, according to the legend, two giants who lived on the hillfort on Mynydd y Gaer above the village jumped down into the fields and left dents where they landed.

The famous cave on the island of Staffa in the Hebrides, Fingal's Cave, was made by a giant, one Fingal who was also said to have made the whole island. Two of Shetland's giants were called Saxi and Herman, and various landscape features are named after them, such as the hills of Saxavord and Hermaness where they lived, a hollow in Saxavord being called Saxi's House, and a chasm in the coastal rocks is Saxi's Kettle because the sea boils and hisses there.

The Avon gorge at Bristol was dug out by a giant called Gorm, who was a famous Somerset giant, but Cheddar Gorge a few miles to the south was dug by the Devil. He did it simply to spoil the smooth green line of the Mendip Hills, and the earth he dug out was thrown all about him, making the islands Steep Holme and Flat Holme in the sea beyond Weston-Super-Mare and the hill of Brent Knoll. The Devil is also credited with excavating a deep chasm up in Shetland, The Holes of Scraada on Mainland. But he had to dig this out as a punishment for wrecking ships on the Ve Skerries, and his groans can still be heard echoing round the chasm. The Devil is also associated with an impressive cave on the north coast of Scotland, Smoo Cave* (Sutherland), where, so it was said, he had a quarrel with one of his pupils, Donald, the Wizard of Reay, which ended with the Devil and the three witches with him blowing holes in the cave roof to escape.

He also had to beat a hasty retreat from the Sussex Downs, where he had been digging the Devil's Dyke, a cleft in the Downs just north of Brighton. He was annoyed that the people of Sussex were converting to Christianity and building churches everywhere, so he decided to dig a channel through the Downs and let the sea in so that they would all be drowned. The earth from his spade flew all around, forming nearby hills like Chanctonbury, Cissbury and Mount Caburn. He had to work quickly, because he had to complete his self-appointed task during the hours of darkness. The noise he was making woke an old woman living in a cottage nearby, and she saw what was going on. So she placed a lighted candle on her windowsill, and held a sieve in front of it so that it looked like a glowing globe. The Devil saw this and, being rather stupid, thought it was the rising sun. Just to complete the illusion, the old woman knocked her cockerel off his perch to make him crow. At which, the Devil flew away, dropping a lump of earth from his cloven hoof which became the Isle of Wight. Or, in another version, he jumped over into Surrey, the hollow he made on landing becoming known as the Devil's Punch Bowl (near Hindhead). He has another Punch Bowl at Cheesefoot Head near Winchester (Hampshire), a place which has in recent years achieved notoriety as a favourite spot for the appearance of crop circles. A seventeenth-century woodcut attributed a similar phenomenon to the Devil. The Devil's Punch Bowl at Kirkby Lonsdale in Cumbria is said to conceal a church which he buried there, and it was said that if you listened carefully with your ear to the ground, you might be able to hear the bells chiming. In Dorset, a hole in the ground near Ibberton is called the Devil's Chimney.

People both real and legendary, as well as assorted monsters, have used caves as homes. In Cumbria, the caves of Isis Parlis on the north bank of the River Eamont near Edenhall were home to the giant Sir Hugh Cesario (also known as Sir Ewen or Isis or Tarquin). The folk hero Guy of Warwick lived in a cave at Guy's Cliffe near Warwick: married to the Earl of Warwick's daughter, his valiant deeds included killing the giant Colbrand, a dragon, a wild boar, and also the Dun Cow, a fairy cow which roamed Dunsmore Heath. She gave her milk freely to everyone, until greedy people milked her into a sieve and wore her out. Thereafter she turned into a monster, and her death at Guy's hands became his best-known exploit, various relics of the Dun Cow in the form of large animal bones being shown at places like Warwick Castle and Coventry in the Middle Ages and later. Guy's cave is still at Guy's Cliffe, and there is a 600-year-old statue of him, 8 feet tall, in the chapel there.

Robin Hood was an even more famous folk hero, and the cave where he is said to have hidden for many years is on the hill called Loxley Edge, at Loxley near Sheffield (South Yorkshire). Loxley has been claimed as Robin Hood's birthplace. Outside the cave, a trough cut from solid rock is said to have been made in order to supply Robin with water. In Shropshire, Kynaston's Cave in the side of Nesscliff Hill was the home of an outlaw, Wild Humphrey Kynaston, who was a sort of Robin Hood figure, robbing the rich to give to the poor. Many tales were told about him locally, and it is likely that they contain a grain of truth, just as the stories of Robin Hood may be based on a real person. Caves in cliffs were often used as refuges by outlaws and criminals, and also by hermits who likewise wished to keep away from other people.

It seems rather less likely that a real person lay behind the scare-stories of Black Annis or Black Anna, a hag with long teeth and nails who ate her human victims, and lived in a cave in the Dane Hills, at that time wasteland but now a part of the city of Leicester. She dug the cave herself with her claws, and its floor was stained with the blood of her victims. She was also seen as a cat, lying in wait in trees, and in more recent times she has changed into a witch living in the cellars of Leicester Castle. No one knows how the legend of Black Annis arose, but she may have connections with the Celtic goddess Anu (or Ana, Dana, Danu), the mother goddess who has here been transformed into a hag. Another cave-dwelling hag was discovered by some men who entered a cave in Rhiwarth rock near Llangynog (Powys). They bought a pound of candles and entered the cave for as far as the candles lasted, and inside they found a hag busily washing clothes in a brass pan. The witch who lived in Wookey Hole (Somerset) was turned to stone when a young monk from Glastonbury sprinkled her with holy water, and she can still be seen there today, standing by the entrance with her demons. She had once been beautiful, but sold herself to the Devil and grew ugly as her wickedness grew.

Also called a witch, though rather more likely to have been a real-life person than the witch of Wookey, was the sixteenth-century prophetess known as Mother Shipton, whose birthplace was said to have been a cave beside the river at Knaresborough (North Yorkshire), now known as Mother Shipton's Cave*. She is said to have predicted the coming of railways, aeroplanes and cars, though some of her prophecies were in fact nineteenth-century forgeries. It is interesting that she should be so closely linked with a cave, because in ancient times oracles which prophesied the future were consulted at caves and grottoes. The legends of King Arthur and his wizard Merlin also mention a cave, the large sea-cave now known as Merlin's Cave at Tintagel* (Cornwall). King Arthur was said to have been born at Tintagel, though according to Tennyson's poem Merlin snatched the baby boy from the sea there. Merlin's ghost is said to haunt the cave.

Dragons and other monsters sometimes took refuge in caves. The Dragon of Wantley had its den in a cave on Wharncliffe Crags near Rotherham (South Yorkshire), until it was killed by More of More Hall, a knight who dressed himself in a suit of armour studded with spikes before setting out to tackle the monster. He finally succeeded in despatching it by a kick up the backside from a spike on the toe of his boot. In Wales, a flying serpent lived in a cave on Moel Bentyrch, a hill near Llanerfyl (Powys). Early in the last century a woman on her way to market saw smoke and fire issuing from the place where its den was, and she didn't stop running until she was some way from the hill. She needn't have worried, because according to tradition the monster had been killed by wrapping red material round a post into which sharp nails had been driven, as with the dragon of Llanrhaeadr-ym-Mochnant which was mentioned in Chapter 2. On the island of Mingulay (Outer Hebrides), on the side facing Pabbay, is a cave known as the Cave of the Monster where a water-horse that was not quite a water-horse was said to live, and in fact it was seen early this century. It followed a boat for a quarter of a mile, and all the crew saw it, describing it as bigger than a land horse and dark grey in colour, but they could not see its feet as it swam. Some lobster fishermen described it as 'just a water-horse, with broad head, fine mane, and eyes like cups'. It swam strongly, and the crew of the boat it was following could

41

not increase the distance between themselves and the monster.

Some caves, caverns and potholes were believed to be bottomless, and also to be the entrance to the Otherworld or Underworld, such as Peak Cavern (Derbyshire). (A rather more colourful name for this gaping hole in the ground was The Devil's Arse.) The story told how a swineherd who was looking for one of his sows which was due to give birth at any time, went into the cave to look for her and after walking for some distance saw light ahead and found himself on a wide plain where the crops were being harvested. He found the missing sow with her piglets, and took her back through the cave, emerging into the winter scene he had recently left. There was no direct suggestion that the country he had visited was Fairyland, though usually the Otherworld that is entered through caves is Fairyland, and there are numerous tales connecting fairies with caves and hollows. In Clwyd, a man returning home from Llangollen late one summer night saw a number of the Little People walking about on Eglwyseg Rocks and he made his way towards them. But they saw him coming and apparently hid behind a large stone. When he got there, he found a hole under the stone through which they had made their way back home. Close by there is a hollow known as Nant-yr-Ellyllon, the Hollow of the Goblins, where the fairies liked to dance. One day a young shepherd boy named Tudur got caught up in a fairy dance from which he could not escape – but the beautiful fairies he thought he had joined turned into ugly goblins with the Devil as fiddler. Only when the lad's master came to look for him next morning, and found him spinning round and round alone in the hollow, was the spell broken.

Of the many other fairy haunts in Wales, two locations with caves where the fairies were said to live were the rock called Craig Rhydderch in the valley of Cwm Mabws, a few miles from Aberystwyth (Dyfed), and the western end of Arennig Fawr near Bala (Gwynedd). The fairies of Craig Rhydderch used to be seen with horses and carriages, and one night some men who had taken horses down to the river for a drink heard a noise on the road and saw passing by a number of little men with little horses and carriages. Shortly after returning home to the farm where they worked, one of their colleagues also came back and said that he too had seen them as he was coming along the same road. Sweet singing used to be heard issuing from the fairy cave on Arennig Fawr, and one of the fairies was a beautiful woman who could be seen climbing the bare slopes of the mountain carrying her harp. One All Hallows Night, a shepherd lad saw scores of fairies singing and dancing on the grass in front of the cave, and he found it difficult to resist joining in with their merry-making. It was said that a harpist was once lured to a cave where the rivers Serw and Conwy join, near Ysbyty Ifan (Gwynedd), by the Little People, who obviously needed him to make music for them – the fairies love singing and dancing. The harpist was never seen again, but his music can sometimes be heard in a field called The Harper's Meadow.

Not all the fairies' caves are in Wales. A cave and waterfall at Chudleigh Rock, and The Pixies' Cave below Sheepstor, Dartmoor, are two caves in Devon where the fairies were said to dwell; while in Durham the Queen of the Fairies was said to live with her court in a cavern at the foot of limestone rocks called Clint's Crags in Weardale. In Worcestershire they had a cave at Osebury (or Rosebury) Rock by the River Teme near Lulsley, and it was said that if a woman should break her peel (long-handled baker's shovel), she should leave it at the cave for the fairies to mend. Also helpful to humans was the goblin Hob Hurst who lived in a cave known as Thirst House below Topley Pike in Deepdale (Derbyshire), because he guarded a healing well, while the hob or boggart who lived in Hob Hole, a cave near Runswick Bay (North Yorkshire), was thought to be able to cure whooping cough, and children were taken by their parents to the Hob Hole in hopes of a cure. They would have to recite a special verse, asking the hob to remove the cough. Another location that was named after its goblin inhabitant was Boggart Hole Clough at Blackley (Greater Manchester). Hobs were kindly spirits, rather like brownies, but the boggart was a mischievous brownie who played tricks on people, of the kind sometimes credited to poltergeists. The area is a wooded valley, where Boggart Hall used to stand, the house being haunted by the boggart, but even though the house has long gone, this 'romantic dell', as it has been described, is still a magical place.

Another example of a fairy cave being linked with healing comes from Scotland, near the point of Kilmuir beyond Kessock Ferry (Ross and Cromarty): the cave was the dripping cave of Craig-a-Chowie. Cattle or children who strayed into the cave were never seen again, and only those people who were in need of its cure were able to enter safely. Water drips from the roof, and people suffering from deafness or earache would lie on the floor and let the water drip first into one ear, then into the other. By following this and other rituals, they hoped to receive a cure. Rituals also had to be followed at Dwynwen's Cave at Tresilian Bay near St Donat's (South Glamorgan), though the participants were not in this instance seeking a cure. Inside the cave was a natural arch called the Bow of Destiny, which a boat could sail over at high tide. It was used for love divination, and young people would try to throw pebbles over the bow. The number of unsuccessful attempts would indicate the number of years until either a single person would marry, or a married person would be free to remarry. St Dwynwen is the Welsh patron saint of lovers.

We have seen that giants, dragons and fairies are among the beings that have made their homes in caves, but by far the greatest number of legends relating to cave occupancy describes the inhabitants as sleeping. They are usually folk heroes, awaiting the call to come to their country's aid, and the hero who features most often is King Arthur. There are at least five locations in Wales alone where he and his knights lie sleeping, including a cave in Craig-y-Ddinas* rock near Glyn-Neath (West Glamorgan) where they are accompanied by a hoard of treasure. Caerleon (Gwent) is one of the places said to be the site of King Arthur's Court, and the still surviving Roman amphitheatre was sometimes called King Arthur's Round Table. The king is said to be sleeping in a cave near Caerleon, and one day a wizard took a farmer inside. They descended a flight of steps where there were bells that the farmer was warned not to touch. After seeing the warriors lying asleep, he accidentally touched one of the bells, whereupon the warriors leapt up and asked whether they were needed now. 'No, sleep on,' replied the wizard, and they fell asleep again. Afterwards, the farmer was unable to find the cave again. There is also said to be a cave in the limestone cliff below Chepstow Castle (Gwent) where King Arthur and his knights lie sleeping.

In the cave called Ogo'r Dinas or Ogof Cil yr Ychen near Llandybie (Dyfed) the sleepers might be King Arthur and his men, or they might be Owain Lawgoch and *his* men, or even Owain Glyndwr and *his* men! (The cave no longer exists, the hill, Craig y Dinas, having been removed by quarrying.) Owain Lawgoch (Owen of the Red Hand) was a real person who was born around 1330 and died in France in 1378, murdered in a conspiracy. He claimed to be a Welsh ruler by ancestry, and a ballad sung in Wales claimed him as the future English king 'Harri'r Nawfed' (Henry the Ninth). King Arthur's men also lie sleeping in a cave in the mountains near Snowdon (Gwynedd), following a battle in the pass called Bwlch y Saethau (Pass of the Arrows) where the king was slain. He was buried under stones, now called Arthur's Cairn, and his men went up to a vast cave above Llyn Llydaw in Cwm Dyli, where they still lie asleep, dressed in their armour and awaiting the second coming of Arthur to restore the crown of Britain to the Welsh. The cave is called Ogof Llanciau Eryri (The Young Men of Snowdonia's Cave), and one day a shepherd rescuing a sheep accidentally found the hidden cave. He looked inside and saw the sleeping men, and he then tried to squeeze inside to investigate further, but he knocked against a bell hanging at the entrance, and it rang loudly, waking the warriors who shouted out and so frightened the shepherd that he was ill ever afterwards, and no one else has ever dared try to find the cave.

Still in Wales, Owain Glyndwr (Owen Glendower), another Welsh folk hero, was said to be sleeping in a cave at Craig Gwrtheyrn (Vortigern's Rock) near Pencader (Dyfed); while in a cave at Penlascarn (Gwent) a farmer found thousands of sleeping warriors and woke one when he stumbled over him. This man was friendly, and told the farmer that they were King George's

45

men, waiting for the blast of a trumpet. Merlin, the bard and prophet from the story of King Arthur, is said to be sleeping in a cave inside Merlin's Hill outside Carmarthen (Dyfed). Carmarthen's Welsh name is Caerfyrddin – Merlin's City – and he is said to have been born there. He was imprisoned by Vivien, to whom he had taught magic spells, and it is said to be still possible to hear his groans.

Elsewhere in Britain, King Arthur and his knights are asleep in a cave under Richmond Castle (North Yorkshire), and also in a cave under the site of the former Sewingshields Castle (Northumberland). A similar story is attached to both these places. At Richmond, a potter named Thompson followed a tunnel into the hillside and found the men asleep at a round table, on which lay a horn and a sword. He picked up one (it varies according to which version you read) and the men began to wake up, so Thompson made a quick departure. As he did so, he heard a voice calling:

> *Potter Thompson, Potter Thompson!*
> *If thou hadst drawn the sword or blown the horn,*
> *Thou hadst been the luckiest man e'er born.*

In the Sewingshields cave, a horn, a sheathed sword and a garter lay on the table, and the right procedure to waken Arthur was to draw the sword, cut the garter, and blow the horn, in that order. A farmer who found the cave cut the garter, whereupon Arthur awoke; but he then put the sword in its sheath and failed to blow the horn, at which Arthur said:

> *O woe betide that evil day*
> *On which this witless wight was born,*
> *Who drew the sword, the garter cut,*
> *But never blew the bugle horn.*

King Arthur and his knights also sleep under the Eildon Hills* (Roxburgh) – or maybe it is Thomas the Rhymer (*the story is told in 'Places to Visit'*) – and a similar tale is told of Alderley Edge*

(Cheshire), where a farmer sold his horse to a man (said to have been Merlin) who took him to a place on the Edge where a rock moved to reveal gates, behind which was a cave with the sleeping men.

Although the names are different, the story told of sleepers in a Scottish cave is similar to one told about the sleeping Arthur. The location is a cave in the cliffs of Barra (Outer Hebrides), where Ossian and his men lie sleeping. Fionn (also known as Finn Mac Cool) and his son Ossian and their men held the same role in the Scottish Highlands as King Arthur and his knights held in England: they were protectors, always ready to defend and assist the people in times of trouble. A fisherman accidentally found the men sleeping in the Barra cave, and picked up a large horn that was lying near them. He blew on it twice, and this woke Ossian who told him to be silent, replace the horn and leave, for their hour had not yet come. 'Harm hast thou done, but hadst thou blown a third time terrible indeed would be that day,' he said, and the fisherman fled. He was never able to locate the cave again.

Finally in this catalogue of cave dormitories, two somewhat different tales, the first from Shropshire. A rock jutting out from Wenlock Edge is known as Ippikin's Rock, Ippikin being a robber-knight who lived with his followers in a hidden cave there, gathering together stolen treasure over many years until one day there was a rock fall which blocked the cave and imprisoned the robbers. However, the cave entrance is in fact still open, and a variant on the tale is that Ippikin fell to his death over the cliff when he was riding home drunk one dark night. It was also said that his ghost could be raised by anyone bold enough to stand on the cliff and cry,

Ippikin! Ippikin!
Keep away with your long chin!

But anyone trying this should be on their guard, because it is also said that the ghost will knock the person who has just insulted him over the cliff to his death. Moving lights seen at night near the cave in the 1880s suggested to folklorist Charlotte Burne that the ghostly robbers were still guarding their treasure. On the Isle of Man, the Devil's Den was a cave at the foot of South Barrule, a mountain in the south of the island, where magicians held people captive. Now it holds a great prince who has been there for hundreds of years, bound by magic spells. Strange noises have been heard coming from the cave, and any animal taken to the entrance will be terrified, with its eyes staring and its hair standing on end.

Frightening things can certainly happen to people who enter caves with bad reputations, and one widespread legend tells how musicians have entered caves and never been seen again, though their music can still be heard. The location for this legend is sometimes an underground passage, but since that is usually a man-made structure we will concentrate here on the cave version, only mentioning passages when they seem from the description to be natural rather than man-made. Such seems to have been the case with a passage which was said to link the islands of Tresco and St Mary's in the Scilly Isles. It was called Piper's Hole, presumably acquiring this name from some tale of a piper venturing into the passage and never coming out at the other end. Dogs were said to have gone through, but to have come out hairless. In Herefordshire, a cleft in some rocks at Orleton was called Palmer's Churn, and a goose which went into the cleft followed an underground passage for about 4 miles. When it came out it cried 'Goose out!', and that is how the place, at Woofferton, got its name of Gauset. (Folklore humour is nothing if not contrived!)

At Trellech in Gwent, it was said that music could be heard coming up from under the ground, and when the meadow was dug an underground cave was discovered where two old men sat playing on a harp and a violin. They had been there for years, only creeping out at night to find food, and they died soon after being discovered and brought out. There is a cave at Criccieth (Gwynedd), called Ogof Du or Black Cave, into which two musicians once disappeared, one playing a pipe and the other a horn. But their music could still be heard 2 miles away, at Braich y Bib (where the piper was heard) and at Braich y Cornor (where the horn was heard), the Welsh names denoting the instruments heard. In South Wales, a fiddler whose candle went out, so that he could never find the exit, is said to haunt Green Bridge Cave near Pendine (Dyfed). He can sometimes be heard, still playing his fiddle.

There are also numerous Piper's Caves in the western Highlands and Islands of Scotland, into which pipers with their dogs disappeared and were never seen again. One was near Boreraig, on Loch Dunvegan (a sea-loch on the Isle of Skye), and although the piper never emerged, it was said that his dog did, coming out exhausted and 'semi-flayed' some time afterwards. Some of the Scottish caves where pipers have disappeared are known as the Caves of Gold, since these caves were also said to be the hiding places of hoards of treasure which no one could ever find. One such was in the mountain Crogary Mor, in North Uist (Outer Hebrides), and in this cave was said to be hidden enough precious metal to fill seven cow-hides. When the folklorist Alasdair Alpin MacGregor was staying on the island, he decided to look for the cave, but when he reached the summit of the mountain he was so entranced by the view that he forgot all about the Caves of Gold.

There are also caves with hidden treasure in England and Wales. In Warwickshire a conical hill near Haselor known as Alcock's Arbour was said to contain a cave where a robber lived, keeping there in an iron-bound chest all the money he had stolen. The chest is said to be still there, guarded by a cock which sits on top of it. An Oxford scholar who came with a key that opened two of the locks, was trying to open the third when the cock attacked him. Also in Warwickshire, a hill called the Mound, near Lindley Hall, similarly conceals treasure in a cave, though this time the robber was Dick Turpin, the famous highwayman. In Devon there is said to be a cave behind a rock wall at Abbot's Weir on the River Tavy at Tavistock. The abbot dreamed about it, and went to find the place: when he struck the rock with his staff, the cave was revealed, with all its treasure. When darkness fell, he loaded as much as he could on to his mule, climbed aboard, and set off back to the abbey. But the mule objected to all the extra weight, and tossed both treasure and abbot into the weir, where he drowned. The treasure in King Arthur's Cave* (near the River Wye, Herefordshire) was, as the name suggests, said to have been hidden there by King Arthur when he was being chased by his enemies, and Merlin later put a spell on the cave so that the treasure would never be found again.

Across the border in South Wales there are several treasure caves, including that in Craig-y-Ddinas* (West Glamorgan) where King Arthur and his warriors also lie sleeping. It was said that a man was shown this treasure by a magician, and told what procedures to follow: he managed to take away some of the treasure, but then he forgot the right procedure and he lost everything. Also in West Glamorgan, on the Gower peninsula, there is a treasure cave on the coast, near Rhossili. It was at the Paviland Caves that the remains of an ancient prehistoric man were found in 1823, originally known as the Red Lady of Paviland until examination showed 'her' to have been a man. He had been buried with a number of ivory ornaments. Does this archaeological discovery have any connection with the legend that the caves are haunted by the ghost of a woman who was looking for treasure but got cut off by the tide and drowned in a storm? Further west, in Dyfed, there is a rock near Llanafan bridge known as Craig yr Ogof (Rock of the Cave), where it was believed that the Romans had hidden treasure. There was also a great deal of treasure in a cave near Devil's Bridge, but it was guarded by a giant bird. Anyone trying to force an entry into the cave would wake the bird, and it would ask in a thunderous voice: 'Are the three mornings one yet?' The correct answer was: 'They are not one, sleep on.' It is not clear whether you had free access to the cave if you gave the right answer; but the cave was opened to all-comers on one day a year, and anyone favoured by the gods could then take what he wanted.

Gwynedd in North Wales seems to have been richly provided with treasure caves. For example, King Arthur's treasure was believed to have been hidden in a coastal cave at Llangwyfan on Anglesey; while a man saw the king's gold crown on a table in a cave by the lake called Marchlyn Mawr, Llandegai. He was a farmer's son, rescuing a sheep from rocks by the lake, when he came across the cave. He entered it at dawn, and in the illuminated interior saw the pearl-encrusted crown which he knew to be King Arthur's. As he reached out to touch it, there was a loud crash and darkness fell. Making his way outside, he saw that the lake was tossing, and a boat with three beautiful women and a terrifying oarsman was coming towards him. He made his escape as quickly as he could, and ever afterwards the mere mention of Marchlyn Mawr drove him into madness. There was also treasure in a cave near Ogwen Lake, discovered by a man exploring there. He tried to take one of the vessels away, but could not lift it, so he decided to return next day with a friend to help him. He concealed the cave entrance with stones, but realized that he might not be able to find it again, so he carefully cut chips off his walking-stick and left them along the route. Next day, he found that all the markers had disappeared, and he could not find the cave. The treasure in the cave called Ogof Dafydd Siencyn (David Jenkin's Cave), between Llanrwst and Trefriw in the Conwy valley, was kept in a huge iron-bound oak chest, guarded by an enormous billy-goat. When a man called Jordan went inside, some time during the reign of Henry the Seventh, the goat threw some gold into a crucible and told him that if he drank the red-hot liquid he would become a man of gold. Presumably he thought that the goat meant he would become rich, but he should have been more cautious, because the goat meant what he said literally, and the man turned to gold. Afterwards he could not leave his cottage for fear someone would steal him! The table heaped with gold and silver which a shepherd found in a cave in Benglog in Llanllechid parish was guarded by a greyhound with fiery eyes. He fetched his brother so that they could enter together and overcome the dog, but he couldn't find the cave again.

One last tale from England: St Cuthbert's Cave* near Hazelrigg (Northumberland), was said to be haunted by a reiver (a raider) who had buried some treasure there, but could never find it again. Perhaps most of the treasure said to be concealed in so many caves nationwide has in fact been mislaid by its owners, or they have for some reason been unable to return and reclaim it, just as the buried treasure sometimes found with the aid of metal-detectors is judged to have been buried for safekeeping in previous centuries but never reclaimed. Whatever the explanation, treasure seems to be an elusive commodity for both owners and seekers.

Springs and Wells

In Britain today, our water supplies are generally taken for granted, especially by city-dwellers who never see or even think about those special places where the earth releases her surplus to feed springs and wells, streams and rivers. It is only in times of drought when we become aware of how reliant we are on natural forces to supply our vital needs that we start to think about where water comes from. But water issuing from the ground is a natural occurrence and our ancestors were much more aware of springs and wells, because they had to visit them often to obtain water for domestic use. Many surviving wells are very ancient, and the first water cults may have originated thousands of years ago. There is much evidence for early veneration of water sources, and well cults were also an important part of the Christian religion. Springs and wells have always been magical places, and despite the neglect which so many have suffered once they lost their vital importance to the community, a large number have been rediscovered and preserved, because many people today can also sense the power of those places where the moving water emerges from the immovable earth. It is as if the tension between the two opposites creates a satisfying balance which humans can appreciate, and which is both calming and invigorating.

In addition to their use as a domestic water supply, many springs (often known as holy wells) were believed to have the power to cure illness, and were visited for that purpose. The most important healing wells were dug out, enlarged, had buildings erected over them, and bathing pools added. Since this book is about the folklore of natural rather than man-made landscape features, such developments take the wells out of our terms of reference. Therefore this chapter is mainly about the origins of springs and wells, for there are a great many stories and legends which explain how they first came into being, as holes in the ground from which water began to flow.

The simplest explanation for the appearance of a spring was that a saint prayed for water and it miraculously appeared. The saint always had a good reason for needing the water. For example, when St Torranan landed on Benbecula (Outer Hebrides) he was very thirsty after his long journey from Ireland. He could find no fresh water, so he prayed for a spring and one appeared at his feet. St Torranan blessed it, drank from it, and after giving thanks he prayed that it might never dry up. It later became a place of pilgrimage. St Margaret's holy well at Binsey (Oxfordshire) is attributed to St Frideswide, a nun who settled at Binsey after having fled from an unwelcome suitor. On her arrival she found a desolate place without water, so she prayed to God and found a pure spring among the grass. Six wells at Stourton (Wiltshire) are said to have arisen when King Alfred prayed for water for his men during battles. St Alban prayed for water to quench his thirst while on his way to his execution on 23 June 303, and thus arose St Alban's Well at St Albans (Hertfordshire). St Edith prayed for water when she was helping to build the church at Stoke Edith (Herefordshire), because it was a long way to the brook to fetch water to mix the mortar, and a vigorous spring began to flow (and still flows) close to the church. Sometimes a spring would appear where needed, but without the saint having recourse to prayer, as for example at

Porthclais, St David's (Dyfed) where Pistyll Dewi (David's Spring) burst forth to be used for baptism.

Saints also produced water by striking the ground with a staff. St Augustine is said to have done this at Cerne Abbas (Dorset) in order to find water for refreshment, and so too did St John of Beverley at Harpham (Humberside) and Archbishop Thomas a Becket at Otford (Kent). On the Isle of Skye where two groups of people were arguing over the use of the local well, St Turog struck the well and caused it to dry up. His anger and the loss of their well caused the parties to appeal to the saint to help them. Separating them into two groups, he struck the ground in front of each group, and two new springs flowed. The well at North Marston (Buckinghamshire) was created by Sir John Schorne, rector during the years 1290–1314, at a time of drought. Moved by the prayers of his congregation, he stuck his staff in the ground and a spring burst forth. Pistyll Baglan, a spring in woods near Llanfaglan church (Baglan, West Glamorgan), was caused to flow by St Baglan when he was building the church and needed water. He struck a rock with a staff (probably the crozier given him by his spiritual master, St Illtyd), the rock split in two, and water flowed from it. But a king with many soldiers then came on the scene and drank all the water. To try and stop them, St Baglan pointed his staff at them, and it began to grow until it was long enough for him to push them away with it. The king apologized and went away, saying he would keep the location of the spring a secret. St Baglan again struck the rock, and the water began to flow again. St David produced a well at Brawdy (Dyfed) with his staff, as described in Rhigyfarch's eleventh-century *Vita-Davidis* (*Life of David*):

> One day a countryman named Terdi with many prayers and entreaties begged his kindly aid, saying: 'Our land is drained dry of water, and we have a toilsome life watering it, because the river is far distant.' The holy father, sympathising with the needs of his neighbours ... went forth and made an opening in the surface of the soil with the point of his staff, and a spring of very clear water gushed out,

bubbling in a continuous flow, which provided the coldest water even in the hot season.

St Milburga's horse created one of the wells dedicated to her, St Milborough's Well at Stoke St Milborough (Shropshire). While escaping from her enemies, she fell from her horse and struck her head on a stone. Two men sowing barley nearby ran to help her, but there was no water to bathe her wound. She commanded her horse to strike the rock with its hoof, and a spring gushed forth. Ffynnon Fair (St Mary's Well) near Aberdaron (Gwynedd) began to flow on the seashore where Our Lady rode out of the sea on a horse, which struck the rock with its hoof. Another well reputedly formed in a similar way is Anne Boleyn's Well at Carshalton (Surrey), which began to flow where Anne Boleyn's horse struck the ground with its hoof. It was not always saints who were responsible for the miraculous flow of water, as the last story shows, and several other wells were also formed in a similar way by secular people. A spring began to flow at Prestwick (Ayr) where Robert the Bruce stuck his spear into the sand when he lay down to rest, and he found that the water from the resulting spring cured his leprosy. Two Sisters Well between Hoton and Wymeswold (Leicestershire) came about as a result of a dream. During a period of drought several hundred years ago, Gertrude and Grace Lacy both dreamt the same dream: that they caused a stream to flow by digging a pilgrim's staff into the earth. Next morning the sisters went to the spot they had dreamt about, accompanied by some villagers, and where they prodded the ground with the staff, a stream began to flow. The villagers built a well at the spot, and the water never dried up. It is possible that tales of saints and other people finding water with staffs may indicate that some form of water divination was being used, rather than pure coincidence or miracles.

There are many legends in which a holy well sprang up where a saint's severed head fell, or where the blood spattered, or simply where his (or her) murder took place or where the body lay. The best-known legend of a decapitation being followed by the appearance of a new spring concerns St Winefride, beheaded by Prince Caradog after she was attacked and possibly raped by him at Holywell (Clwyd). Her uncle St Beuno was on hand to replace the severed head, and the famous holy well of St Winefride* has developed from the spring which flowed where her head came to rest after rolling downhill (*see plate 10*). St Lludd was beheaded at Pencefngaer (Powys) in the same circumstances as St Winefride, Penginger Well now marking the spot where her head fell. Digwg's Well near Clynnog (Gwynedd) marked the place where the daughter of Ynyr, King of Gwent, was beheaded by her husband, who was ashamed that he had pretended to be a nobleman when in fact he had no home to take her to. She was discovered by a shepherd, who fetched St Beuno (who founded his main monastery at Clynnog Fawr and was therefore close by) and he joined her severed head to her body. Women were also beheaded for various other reasons. The female Christian saint Columba had a pagan lover who, when she refused to renounce Christianity, beheaded her at Ruthvoes (Cornwall), where her holy well began to flow. St Sidwell was beheaded in the eighth century on the order of her jealous stepmother, who persuaded her serfs to cut off Sidwell's head with their scythes, and where her blood spattered a spring began to flow, known as St Sidwell's Well, in Exeter (Devon). At St Osyth (Essex), a well flowed where the seventh-century abbess, St Osyth, was attacked and beheaded by Danes who raided her convent. According to the legend, she picked up her severed head and carried it to the nearest church, where she died, and there was at one time a belief that her ghost haunted both the well and the church.

Two male saints who were beheaded, with holy wells resulting from their deaths, were St Decuman and St Justinian. Decuman was a Welsh saint who crossed to Somerset and established a hermitage at Watchet, but he was attacked and beheaded by the local pagans, St Decuman's Well springing up where his head fell (or, in another version, the well was already there and St Decuman washed his severed head in its water). He gathered up his head and went back to Wales, where another St Decuman's Well arose near Rhoscrowther church (Dyfed) where he put his head down. Also in Dyfed, St Justinian's Well* near St Davids, marks the place where the saint put down his head. He was beheaded by his servants on Ramsey Island and a healing well flowed where he was beheaded; then he picked up his head and took it a short distance across the sea to the mainland, being buried in St Justinian's Chapel close to the well (later he was buried with St David).

There are many holy wells which according to legend began to flow where saints died or were murdered. St Oswald's Well is located where the saint died in 642 following a battle with Penda, King of Mercia, at Winwick (Cheshire), and according to the sixteenth-century antiquary John Leland, his death also led to the formation of another St Oswald's Well, at Oswestry (Shropshire): 'an eagle snatched away an arm of Oswald from the stake, but let it fall in that place where now the spring is.' St Edward's Well arose at Wareham (Dorset) where St Edward the Martyr, King of England, died in 979; while in Norfolk, St Withburga's Well* in East Dereham churchyard marks the place where the saint lay buried for more than 300 years, before her body was removed by the Abbot of Ely in the tenth century to a grave in Ely Cathedral. In other instances, wells sprang up where saints' bodies were only briefly laid during their last journey. Two wells mark the death of Ethelbert, King of East Anglia, who was murdered by order of King Offa of Mercia while Ethelbert, a suitor of Offa's daughter, was his guest. Miracles were soon reported at Ethelbert's grave at Marden* (Herefordshire), and when the body was removed to Hereford, a spring began to flow in the empty grave. At the place in Hereford where the body briefly lay, St Ethelbert's Well began to flow, and King Offa, regretting the murder, had a shrine erected to Ethelbert's memory in 795, on the site of which now stands Hereford Cathedral, of which Ethelbert is the patron saint. The site of his well can still be seen near the entrance to Castle Green, not far from the cathedral, though water no longer flows here.

Two wells also originated from the murder of the child-king Kenelm of Mercia early in the ninth century. He was murdered in the Clent Hills (Worcestershire) at the instigation, so it was said, of his elder sister Quendreda, but from his severed head a dove flew up and away to Rome, where it dropped a scroll at the Pope's feet. This was deciphered, and was found to contain the message:

In Clent Cow-pasture under a thorn
Of head bereft lies Kenelm, King born.

The body was found and taken away to Winchcombe (Gloucestershire) for burial, where Kenelm's father King Kenulf had founded an abbey. At the spot in the Clent Hills were the body had lain (behind St Kenelm's church, Romsley), a spring began to flow, which can still be seen, and another arose near Winchcombe, where the body was rested before burial. St Walstan, son of King Benedict of East Anglia who became a patron saint of agricultural workers and sick animals, died in 1016 in Norfolk while engaged in his chosen work as a farmhand, but he had foreseen his own death and asked that his body be placed on a cart and the two oxen which drew it should be allowed to go where they wished. They passed through Costessey Wood, and at the point where they briefly stopped on a hilltop, St Walstan's Well arose. They stopped again at Bawburgh, where a second spring began to flow (still to be seen on a farm below Bawburgh church), and Walstan was buried not far away, the church being built over his grave. His well is blessed annually on or near his feast-day (30 May). In Gwent, St Tewdric's Well at Mathern (near the church) began to flow when the cart carrying Tewdric, a King of Gwent and Glamorgan, reached this spot. He had been wounded in battle, and when the well began to flow, his followers were able to wash his wounds. He died close by, having asked that a church be built where he died.

There are many other well creation legends which do not involve the deaths of saints, though saints often feature in the stories. St Maughold's Well sprang up on the Isle of Man at the place where St Maughold's horse's knee touched the ground as horse and saint crossed over from Ireland. A similar story is told of another Manx well, this one having three names – St Patrick's Well, Blessed Well, and Well of the Silver, near Peel. St Patrick was being chased by a sea monster as he came to the island and he sent his horse up a steep hill in order to escape. They rested at the top and a spring flowed at their feet. In an alternative story, the spring flowed where St Patrick made the sign of the cross on the ground. In Wales, St David's Well was actually located inside a cottage in Llanddewibrefi parish (Dyfed), and was said to have burst forth to mark the spot where the saint restored the cottager's son to life. The St David's Well at Brawdy (Dyfed) flowed where the saint's tears fell; and St German's Well at Rame Head (Cornwall) likewise fell where the saint shed tears. The rocks were said to have wept in sympathy with his suffering, after his persecutors tried to drive him from the place. In Scotland, a well sprang up where a saint threw her eyes. St Medana's Well is on the shore of Monreith Bay at Glasserton (Wigtown) (100 yards north-west of the old church) and was long known for its ability to cure whooping cough. St Medana (or Modwenna) used a rock as a boat to sail here from Whithorn, and she was followed by an unwelcome suitor. Realizing that he was captivated by her beautiful eyes, Medana plucked them out and threw them at his feet. After he had left, she bathed her face in the water which had started to flow, and by a miracle her sight was restored.

Sometimes there were said to be visible signs of a saint's presence at a well in the form of his chair, or bed, footprints or fingerprints. By Our Lady's Well at Stow (Midlothian) was once a large stone bearing a footprint of the Virgin Mary, while it was St Patrick's knees and left hand which were said to have left marks on a rock in a quarry at Portpatrick (Wigtown) where there was also a St Patrick's Well. St Columba's footprints (though he seems to have had two right feet!) are incised on a rock near the holy well and ancient chapel of Keil in Kintyre (Argyll), but these footprints, and others like them, may have been carved for use in the inauguration ceremonies of kings and chieftains. In a rock basin beside St Tydecho's Well, high up in the hills above Llanymawddwy (Gwynedd), can be seen the saint's fingerprints. People seeking a cure at St Madron's Well at Madron (Cornwall) would as part of the ritual sleep in St Madron's Bed close by; while on the Isle of Man women wishing for children would drink the water of St Maughold's Well and sit in the saint's chair.

Rituals such as those mentioned above are really out of the scope of this book, but much more information on the way in which people used holy wells can be found in our earlier book, *Sacred Waters: Holy Wells and Water Lore in Britain and Ireland*. Details of unusual qualities possessed by the water in some springs and wells are relevant to this book, however, and we start with the belief that some wells were bottomless. Examples are Ffynnon Ddol, Abergele (Clwyd), and a spring in Alrewas Hayes (Staffordshire). Hell's Cothern (Cauldron) near Bingfield (Northumberland) no longer exists, but in its time it was 'an upshot spring of considerable volume', supposedly unfathomable. The force of the water made it appear as if boiling, this being attributed to its 'connection with subterranean fire', that is, Hell. There was a story that a team of oxen and the cart to which they were yoked once became unmanageable and dashed down the bank towards the Cothern. During the descent the cart's pole dug into the ground, and a well was formed at that spot. The oxen left a furrow in the ground as they hurtled towards the Cothern, and when they reached it, the whole lot, oxen, cart and driver, were drowned. Shortly afterwards, the horns of the oxen were thrown up by the force of the water, but nothing was ever seen of the rest.

Another boiling well was the Silver Nut Well at Meadowhaugh near Otterburn (Northumberland). It got its name from the debris of trees and hazel-nuts perfectly preserved that were said to be brought up in the water, the nuts silvered by a chemical action of the water. As in the previous account, a man, horse, and cart loaded with hay were said to have once disappeared into the Silver Nut Well, and also into Ffynnon Ddol mentioned earlier. Other substances supposedly thrown out from wells include small bones, the size of sparrows' bones, reportedly sprayed out with the water from the Well in the Wall, in Checkley parish (Staffordshire), in every month except July and August. The Well of Kilbar on Barra (Outer Hebrides) was said to throw out the embryos of cockles, which made their way somehow to the sandy beaches where they grew to full-size cockles. Another Barra well, near Tangstill, threw out barley grain in July and August in a fertile year.

On rare occasions wells have produced milk, or a milk-like substance. This is said to have happened at St Winefride's Well, Holywell (Clwyd), for three days after the saint's death, while at St Illtyd's Well on Gower (West Glamorgan), in a year unknown, a copious stream of milk was seen to flow by a number of witnesses. St Llawddog milked a cow over a well on Bardsey Island (Gwynedd), so the well then produced milk instead of water for his visitors. The water of Ffynnon Cegin Arthur (the Well of Arthur's Kitchen) in Llanddeiniolen parish (Gwynedd) had an oily appearance, said to have been caused by animal fat from Arthur's kitchen; while the oil which appears in the Balm Well at Liberton, Edinburgh (Midlothian) was said to have originated with some of the healing oil which seeps from St Catherine of Alexandria's relics, perhaps dropped into the Balm Well when angels were carrying her body from Alexandria to Mount Sinai via Scotland.

Several wells produced a substance which was described as blood, sometimes that of a saint, as at Canterbury Cathedral (Kent) where the water of a healing well in the precincts was said to be stained red with the blood of the murdered St Thomas a Becket. One legend claimed that the blood-stained dust from the cathedral was thrown into the well after the murder. Murders are a frequent explanation for red wells: two Breconshire (Powys) wells flowed with blood after the beheading of princes, while further north Collen's Well near Llangollen (Clwyd) became red when St Collen washed himself there after killing a giantess who lived nearby and had a habit of killing and eating passing travellers. Blood Well at Llanyblodwel (Shropshire) was named from a great massacre when bodies were thrown into the well; while Bloodstone Well near Brading (Isle of Wight) has reddish pebbles which took their colour from the blood of the Saxons and Danes who fought a great battle nearby. Red marks on pebbles were sometimes seen as saint's blood: of St Winefride at

Holywell (Clwyd), and of St Michael at Rockfield (Gwent). Reddish water in Chalice Well, Glastonbury* (Somerset) was from Christ's blood in the chalice or Holy Grail thought to be hidden here. It is in fact the chalybeate (impregnated with iron salts) water which appears reddish.

Other unusual physical properties of springs and wells include never freezing or never running dry, and sometimes these phenomena are found together, as at St Andrew's Well at Kirkandrews-on-Eden (Cumbria), which was 'not affected by the most intense frost or the longest drought'. Some wells had water which ebbed and flowed: the Ebbing and Flowing Well at Giggleswick (North Yorkshire) was named for this peculiarity. It still exists at the foot of Giggleswick Scar, but no longer ebbs and flows. Ffynnon Leinw, Cilcain (Clwyd) also used to ebb and flow, twice daily, but again no longer does so. It was thought that the phenomenon was somehow caused by the tides, though Tobar na Bile (Well of the Margin) at Inverliever (Argyll) was believed to ebb and flow with the fortunes of the local lairds. The 'flaming well' at Wigan (Greater Manchester) was probably unique, the explanation for this phenomenon, recorded in 1658 and 1739, being that gas from the coal mines escaped through the same rock fissures as the water, and when the gas was lit, it burned very close to the flowing water, making it seem that the water was on fire. It is recorded that the water got so hot, eggs could be boiled in it. One unusual quality possessed by a number of wells, but best witnessed at the Dropping Well, Dripping Well or Petrifying Well at Knaresborough* (North Yorkshire), is the apparent ability to turn objects to stone. The water at these wells contains carbonate of lime which, when deposited on plants round a well, or any other objects, hardens them and makes them seem to be made of stone.

Some wells made strange noises, which sounded like drumming. The most famous of these was the Drumming Well at Oundle (Northamptonshire), and the noise was said to be prophetic. The drumming was said to be linked to important national events, such as the death of King Charles the Second, and great battles. The drumming noise in the well at Harpham (Humberside) was said to announce a death in the local St Quintin family: an ancestor had killed a drummer boy by accidentally knocking him into the well, so it was said, this event being witnessed by the boy's mother. She said: 'Squire St Quintin, you were the friend of my boy, but from your hand his death has come. Therefore, whenever a St Quintin, Lord of Harpham, dies, my poor boy shall beat his drum at the bottom of this fatal well.' St Helen's Well at Rushton Spencer (Staffordshire) would periodically run dry, and this was believed to predict some national calamity. The well had run dry before the outbreak of the Civil War, at the beheading of King Charles the First, at the outbreak of the First World War, and at other times. Various other wells likewise were in some way able to make predictions, such as the future price of corn.

Some wells and springs are guarded by – or haunted by – beings: monsters, fairies, witches, ghosts, spirits . . . Many of these may have been memories of pre-Christian water divinities: other water sources such as rivers and streams (*Chapter 2*) and pools and lakes (*Chapter 6*) also have many legends of goddesses, which were usually awesome and often frightening beings. It's probably impossible to know which legends genuinely are memories of ancient divinities, and which are invented stories, and your assessment of them will depend on whether or not you believe that it is possible for people's religious beliefs of over two thousand years ago to have survived to the present day in the form of myths and legends. The following monster stories are likely to be no more than fairly recent inventions, in two cases probably suggested by existing place names. Nine Maidens Well at Kirkton of Strathmartine (Angus) was the place where a dragon killed eight daughters of a farmer. The cries of the ninth were heard by her lover called Martin, who after a hard-fought struggle managed to slay the monster. Martin's Stone is now said to mark the spot: but it is a Pictish stone carved with strange creatures, and this plus the nearby place-name Baldragon may have provided a local story-teller with the idea for a good story.

The Leicestershire place-name of Griffydam may have

suggested to another story-teller that a griffin had at some time lurked in these regions. At any rate, the story now told is that the communal well suddenly became home to a monster, and no one could scare it away, until a knight rode into the village looking for water for his horse. When told about the problem with the well, he went to look, and saw the griffin enjoying the afternoon sun. The knight called for bow and arrows, and then, just as the griffin was waking up and yawning, the knight shot an arrow straight into its mouth and killed it. It was said that its skin was taken to nearby Breedon church and hung over the church door. In Northumberland, three wells on the bank of the River Hart at Longwitton were said to be guarded by an invisible dragon. Sir Guy of Warwick, whom we met in Chapter 3, came to fight it, and forced it to appear in visible form. However the fight was not an easy one, for every time the dragon was wounded it would dip its tail into a well and regain its strength. So Sir Guy had to manoeuvre himself into a position between the dragon and the well before he was able to kill it. Other wells where dragons lay curled up included Grinston Well in Brawdy parish (Dyfed), the Well of the Maidens (Aberdeen) and the Serpent Well (Ffynnon Sarff) in Llanengan parish (Gwynedd).

Some wells were fairy dwellings, or doorways into their underworld homes, which were normally closed to humans, unless one accidentally 'turned the key'. A youth cutting turf with other people on the moorland at Cwmtirmynach north of Bala (Gwynedd) washed his face in a fairy well at dinner-time, then went to fetch the food. But he never returned, nor could his friends find the food. A wise man who came to the neighbourhood told them to go to the place of his disappearance on the night of the full moon in June, and they would see him dancing with the fairies. They did as he suggested, and saw the moor covered with thousands of fairies singing and dancing, and the missing man was among them. They grabbed him and managed to pull him away. But he disappeared on another occasion, only to return at full moon in June with a beautiful wife whose origins were unknown, though everyone believed her to be one of the fairyfolk. Some fairy wells were given appropriate names, such as Fairies' Well near Hardhorn (Lancashire) or Fairy Well at Laugharne (Dyfed). Sometimes the fairies controlled a well's powers and could cure illness and grant wishes; and sometimes people threw gifts of pins and buttons into wells for the fairies. Bits of cheese were dropped into the water of the Cheese Well, Minchmoor (Peebles), for the fairies that were believed to live there. A bowl of milk or other offering was left at the Well of the Spotted Rock (Inverness) by any woman who believed her baby was a changeling. She would also leave the child there overnight, hoping that when she returned in the morning, she would find her own healthy child, the changeling having been taken back by the fairies.

Many wells and springs have a reputation for being haunted, though the nature of the haunting ranges from a vague sense of the supernatural, to a 'white lady' ghost who might be the shadow of a water goddess or merely wreaths of mist appearing to take human shape, to a reliable recent first-hand report. Many cases are on the borderline, possibly having some factual basis, but more likely wholly legendary. A few examples will show the wide variety of ghostly phenomena that wells have attracted. A phantom hand was sometimes seen stretched over people drinking at the Well of the Outstretched Hand near Dores (Inverness), and this was said to belong to the spirit of the well. The white lady which haunted St Julian's Well at Wellow (Avon) was the family ghost of the Hungerfords who lived in the Manor House, and she would appear beside the well whenever a calamity was about to befall the family. In Northumberland, Meg of Meldon, said to be a witch and a miser, had placed a bull's hide full of gold in a well near Meldon Tower, and after her death her ghost haunted the well. A former servant at Waddow Hall (Lancashire) haunted Peg o' Nell's Well nearby: she was said to have died while fetching water from the well, after her master expressed a wish that she might fall and break her neck. Gwenno's Well at Cynwyl Gaio (Dyfed) is haunted by Gwenno in the form of a wreath of mist hanging over the rocks. She was taken by spirits while exploring caves nearby. There are several tales of Welsh wells where ghosts appeal to be released from bondage, but human attempts to help end in failure. One well with this legend was St David's Well at Henfynuw (Dyfed) where a ghost was imprisoned. He called for help to an old man visiting the well one Midsummer's Eve, and the old man saw a hand reaching from under the well. The voice asked him to clasp it and hold tight, but it slipped free and as it vanished the ghost cried that he was bound for another fifty years.

Water sources, whether rivers and streams, wells and springs, or pools and lakes, can be seen as mysterious and ever-changing, places where this world and the hidden otherworld meet, which is why they attract so many legends about insubstantial water goddesses, fairies, ghosts and shape-changing spirits like kelpies; in contrast to the hills and mountains, caves and hollows, rocks and stones – solid, unchanging places which are the haunts of giants and devils and larger-than-life folk heroes.

Cliffs and Coasts

Britain is an island with 6,000 miles of coastline, and a rich folklore has grown up around the many caves, coves, sandbars, bays, cliffs, rocks, and offshore islands. The same players whom we have already met in earlier chapters naturally reappear in these tales: the Devil, various giants, witches, King Arthur, fairies, and assorted monsters, ghosts and mermaids. Sometimes they are responsible for creating a notable feature, and sometimes they simply haunt it. But whatever the tale may be, collectively they show that our ancestors saw Britain's coastline differently from the way we usually view it today. Now we see sandy beaches ideal for relaxation, or we see areas of outstanding natural beauty and wildlife interest that need to be protected from exploitation. Our ancestors saw none of these things, their vision was more elemental: they saw powerful forces at work which they did not understand, and which were likely to be of a supernatural nature, and their imaginations went to work to weave a magical web of legends around the majestic coastal features.

Islands had varying origins, but giants were often responsible, and the Scottish Outer Hebrides were all that remained of a dead giant. He was half serpent and half man, he had nine heads, and he lived in a castle on Stack Rock which was the only island at that time west of the Minch. He would raid islands such as Skye and Raasay, Eigg and Rhum, and take maidens for his meals. The betrothed of one of these maidens enlisted the aid of a friendly water-horse, which carried the young man off to tackle the giant. Together they cut off eight of his heads and then stabbed him in the heart, but a problem arose in disposing of the body, for there was nowhere to bury it, and it was too big to sink underwater. So they left it where it lay, and soon it was nothing but bare bones, these in time turning into cliffs and rocks, and gathering a covering of earth. The giant's remaining head forms the Butt of Lewis and his feet the cliffs of South Berneray, with his body in between these two extremes. His other heads became the islands of Killegray, Pabbay, Taransay, Grimsay, Vallay, Mingulay, Eriskay, and Berneray. Further south, the islands of Flat Holm and Steep Holm in the Bristol Channel were the bones of a Somerset giant called Gorm, who fell over while running away from someone. However another story describes these two islands as soil thrown away by the Devil when he was digging out Cheddar Gorge.

Some islands appear and disappear, like the one off Port Soderick (Isle of Man) which used to appear once every seven years. It had originally been a normal island, until the people who lived there somehow insulted the great magician Finn Mac Cool. In revenge he turned the people to stone and sent the island to the bottom of the sea, only allowing it to come to the surface for thirty minutes every seven years. The spell could be broken if, during that thirty minutes, someone placed a Bible on any part of the island while it was above the sea. One fine moonlit night at the end of September, a girl called Nora, who knew of the legend, was walking with her lover along the bay when she saw something slowly rising from the water, and she realized that it must be the enchanted island. She rushed home shouting for the Bible, and then hurried back to the beach, but she was just in time to see the island slowly sinking into the sea again.

Other enchanted islands are the so-called Green Islands of the Sea, which are said to lie off the south Pembrokeshire/ Carmarthenshire coast (Dyfed), and to be visible only occasionally to people. It was said that sailors had sometimes landed on them, only to see the land disappear before their eyes when they returned to their boats. Fairies lived on the islands, and regularly went to the mainland, through an undersea tunnel, to do their shopping in the markets of Milford Haven and Laugharne, though they were often invisible to humans. They never spoke, but paid for their goods with silver pennies. In the late nineteenth century it was reported in a local newspaper that a sea-captain called John Evans had, earlier that century, seen a floating island that he knew should not be there, while he was passing Grassholme Island. It was a few feet below the surface of the water, and looked like a grassy meadow, with the grass waving as the sea rippled over it.

There was said to be a way that one could see the enchanted islands off Dyfed, and that was to take a turf from St David's churchyard and stand on it. One man who did this, immediately put to sea intending to sail to the islands, but they disappeared and he could not find them. He tried again, and failed again. The third time, he took the turf into his boat and stood on it until he reached the islands. The story did not tell whether he ever returned, but it was believed that anyone who was able to visit the islands would find on his return that centuries had passed, although he thought he was only away for a few hours. This is the usual result of visiting Fairyland or the Otherworld, and the Green Islands of the Sea are similar to other legendary islands such as Tir Nan Og (the Celtic Otherworld which lay beyond and under the sea) and Hy Breasil (the enchanted island said to be sometimes seen to the west of Ireland from the coast of Galway). Back in Pembrokeshire, someone who visited Garn Fawr near Fishguard on a sunny summer's evening intending to watch the sunset, saw 'a striking mirage'. It was 'a stretch of country similar to a landscape in this country. A farmhouse and outbuildings were seen . . . [with] fences, roads, and gateways . . . but in the haze it looked more like a panoramic view than a veritable landscape', and he thought that similar mirages could have caused the people of earlier centuries to think they were seeing 'the abode of the fairies'.

Ynys Enlli or Bardsey Island, off the Lleyn Peninsula (Gwynedd), is a sacred place of pilgrimage where there was once a Celtic monastery, and where twenty thousand monks and pilgrims are said to be buried, giving the island its other name of the Isle of the Twenty Thousand Saints. Ghostly monks seen on the shore are a sign that storms and shipwrecks are imminent. Merlin, the magician of the Arthurian sagas, is said to be sleeping on Bardsey in an underground chamber, surrounded by the Thirteen Treasures of Britain and assorted ancient relics, and he has the power to crown Arthur as king when he awakens. In another version of the story, Merlin is in an invisible house of glass, with nine companions.

The most isolated piece of land in Great Britain must surely be Rockall, an uninhabited rock out in the Atlantic Ocean, 240 miles west of the Outer Hebrides. Rockall was believed to be the Celtic Paradise, or Tir Nan Og, the Isles of the Blest, which lay somewhere out to the west. Tir Nan Og was said to be sometimes visible from the Isle of Skye, and the folklorist Otta F. Swire believes she saw it in 1960. She was driving from Uig to Duntulm when she saw an island where no island should have been. It was 'a soft blue touched with rose', and had the shape of Fladda, but was nearer than that island. She took a photograph and continued on her way. Coming back an hour later, she saw Fladda but not the other island. The photograph showed only Fladda. Another magical island is Lundy off the north Devon coast; its name means 'puffin island' in Norse, and today it is a bird sanctuary. In legend it is the entrance to Annwn, the Celtic version of Hades, the land of the dead. This is not the same as Hell, which is the place of punishment, and being generally feared has given its name to dangerous coastal features like Hell's Mouth near Portreath (Cornwall).

Islands there are aplenty around Britain's coast: and some of these may be the highest points of larger stretches of land now submerged. Both in fact and in legend there are many 'lost lands' around England and Wales, and even today there are places where the coastline is being steadily eroded by the sea. Coastal defences to protect the land from erosion and inundation have been set up in many vulnerable places, but still the sea takes its toll, as it has done for centuries. The most famous 'lost land' must be Lyonesse, which in tradition (and maybe also in reality) once existed to the south and west of Land's End (Cornwall), the present Scilly Isles being the hilltops of Lyonesse. There is some documentary evidence to support the reality of Lyonesse, and stone walls and huts and other remains have been found below the high-water mark in the Scillies. In Mount's Bay in the far south-west of Cornwall tree stumps have been found below sea-level, showing that the area is a submerged forest, and the old Cornish name of St Michael's Mount*, a large offshore rock in Mount's Bay, is Carrick Luz en Cuz, or 'the ancient rock in the wood'. This must be an ancient name, because the Mount has been an island since at least 300 BC. Lyonesse is mentioned in some Arthurian tales, though the location is unclear. According to legend, it was inundated very swiftly and unexpectedly. Old fishermen used to say that on clear moonlit nights they could see the roofs of houses and churches under the water, and hear the church bells ringing. The church bells of drowned Dunwich churches (Suffolk) were also said to be heard from time to time, warning of impending storms. Dunwich was once a major port and the capital of East Anglia, but gradual erosion over the four-teenth to twentieth centuries has resulted in most of the town being lost to the sea, including nine churches.

Wales has lost more land to the sea than any other part of Britain, and three major kingdoms were submerged: Cantre'r Gwaelod in Cardigan Bay, Caer Arianrhod to the south of Anglesey, and Llys Helig on the north-west coast. Cantre'r Gwaelod is thought to have covered an area of 40 by 20 miles, from the River Teifi to Bardsey Island, and one of the churches that served it can still be seen in the sand dunes at Llandanwg (Gwynedd). Remains in the form of causeways may confirm the existence of the now-sunken land. Sarn Badrig, apparently a stone wall 24 feet thick, runs out into the sea from Mochras, a few miles south of Harlech (Gwynedd), extending for nearly 20 miles and in some people's eyes a man-made structure, although the 'causeways' are thought by geologists to be natural features. There are other 'causeways' running into the sea further south, and the remains of submerged forests have also been found. Cantre'r Gwaelod is thought to have been submerged in a sudden disaster, and according to legend one of the men in charge of the floodgates failed to perform his duties one night because he was drunk, with the result that the sea burst in and overwhelmed the sea wall.

Caer Arianrhod further north was a town half a mile off the coastal hillfort of Dinas Dinlle (Gwynedd), possibly submerged in the sixth century. It is claimed that the remains of stone walls just below the surface of the sea can be seen at low tide. According to legend, some women had come out of the town to fetch food or water, and while they were away the place was swallowed up by the sea as punishment for the evil way of life that was followed there. The third drowned land was Tyno Helig, which covered an area about 12 by 8 miles between Bangor, Puffin Island (off Anglesey) and the Great Orme. When the Lavan Sands are uncovered at low tide, tree roots have been found. The lord of Tyno Helig was Helig ap Glannawg, whose palace was Llys Helig to the west of Conwy, and its ruins are said to be visible about 2 miles out to sea. The lord heard a ghostly voice prophesying vengeance, but when he asked when this would happen, he was relieved to be told 'In the time of children, grandchildren, great-grandchildren, and great-great-grandchildren'. Many years on, when all his descendants were at a banquet in the palace, a servant went into the cellar to fetch wine and found that it was under water, and fish were swimming about. Before the news could be passed on, a great wave swept over the palace, and next morning Tyno Helig had disappeared. All along the north coast of Wales are various relics of former lands now under the sea; while on the south coast also there are known sites of submerged forests. The whole coastline of Wales is now very different from what it once was.

Many of the changes that have been wrought by natural forces

73

at that point where the sea washes against the land have in legend been attributed to giants, devils, and other larger-than-life figures. Some unusually shaped rocks are said to be people who were turned to stone, as for example the pinnacle called Lot's Wife which was once a part of the Needles of the Isle of Wight. She can no longer be seen, however, having fallen into the sea in 1764. The Parson and Clerk Rocks are still in existence, though, on the north Devon coast at Dawlish. The story told to explain the name is that an ambitious priest, wanting to become bishop after the death of the then incumbent who was ill, frequently visited the sick man at Dawlish where he was living, accompanied by his clerk. One night they lost their way in a storm, and the priest shouted at the clerk, 'I would rather have the Devil himself, than you, for a guide!' As he said this, a horseman rode past and offered to lead them to Dawlish. They followed him thankfully, and a long journey ensued, by the end of which they were very hungry. Arriving at a mansion, they accepted the horseman's offer of a meal. While they were eating, news came that the bishop was dead, and the priest became anxious to depart, wanting to be available for the vacant post. The priest and his clerk mounted their horses and urged them on, but the horses refused to move. 'Devil take the brutes!' cried the priest. 'Thank you, sir,' said their host. 'Gee up!' The horses then galloped at breakneck speed for the cliffs and went straight over the edge, where they still are today. Further north, in south-west Scotland, the rocks in Luce Bay (Wigtown) known as the Scares were said to be St Medana's eyes, which she plucked out and threw away, rather than marry an unwanted suitor.

Whereas St Medana threw her eyes across the sea out of dire necessity, giants seem to have positively enjoyed throwing rocks about. The Ve Skerries, rocky islets north-west of Papa Stour (Shetland), were boulders thrown there in play by the giant Atla, while in both Orkney and Shetland there are many rocks named from giants' activities. For example, Saxi's Baa is a boulder in the sea off Hermaness (Shetland) which Saxi, one of the giants of Unst, threw at Herman, who was another Unst giant, when they were arguing over sharing an ox (or a whale) they were boiling in

Saxi's cauldron. Herman threw a rock back at Saxi, and that is now called Herman's Helyak and is embedded in the cliffs of Saxavord. In the Pentland Firth, the sea between the Orkneys and Caithness, there is a whirlpool called the Swelkie, and this was said to be the salt-grinder or magic quern Grotti, used by the female giants called Fenia and Menia, the circle of the whirlpool being the rotating millstone.

At the opposite end of the country, there are numerous giant tales located round the rocky coasts of Devon and Cornwall. At Plymouth Hoe (Devon) was told the story of Gogmagog's Leap, the name given to a cliff from where the giant Gogmagog was thrown to his death following a wrestling match with Corineus, Duke of Cornwall. There was at one time a figure of a giant cut into the chalk of the Hoe, but it no longer survives, and no one knows when it was first cut. It was said to represent Gogmagog, though according to one reference there were once *two* figures, named Gog and Magog. It (or they) was destroyed in the reign of Charles the Second when the Citadel was built, and during the construction gigantic jaws and teeth were allegedly found, and of course identified as those of Gogmagog. A coastal chasm near Portreath (Cornwall) was known as Ralph's Cupboard, where a giant called Wrath lived (Ralph was probably adapted from Wrath, and the latter was more likely to have meant 'giant' rather than being the name of one). The giant would capture fishing boats and pull them into his den, throwing away the skinny sailors and keeping the fatter ones for his dinner. Those ships in water too deep for him to wade in, he would sink by throwing rocks at them, and these missiles survive as a reef. The roof of the Cupboard collapsed after the giant's death, leaving an open chasm.

The giant Bolster was able to stand with one foot on St Agnes Beacon and the other on Carn Brea (Cornwall), those two peaks being about 6 miles apart. He fell in love with the virtuous St Agnes, and followed her around sighing and groaning and endlessly proclaiming his love. Unable to persuade him to desist, she asked him to prove his love for her by filling with his blood a certain hole in the cliff at Chapel Porth. Bolster readily agreed, but what he did not know was that the hole was bottomless. Using a knife, he opened a vein in his arm and held it over the hole, expecting it to fill quickly, but several hours later the hole was not yet filled, and Bolster could not see that his blood was pouring into the sea. Eventually he fainted from exhaustion, and being unable to stop the bleeding, he died. To this day a trail of red marks the place where the giant's blood flowed. A similar tale is told of a giant from Goran, also in Cornwall, who fell ill and called the doctor, who, thinking that here was a chance to get rid of the terror of the neighbourhood, told him that he must be bled, and that a large hole in the cliff must be filled with the blood. The giant at first felt relief from the blood-letting and so allowed it to continue, and when he became too weak to resist, the doctor kicked him over the cliff and killed him. The promontory called Dodman, or the Dead Man, is said to take its name from this event.

Churches on high places are often dedicated to St Michael, his most famous shrine in western Europe being Mont-Saint-Michel in northern France, where an abbey was founded in the tenth century to commemorate a vision of the saint. This is the mother house of the religious community that was set up on St Michael's Mount*, a small rocky island off the south coast of Cornwall (*see plate 14*). Here also a vision of St Michael was reportedly seen. The folklore explanation for this prominent coastal feature is that it was built by the giant Cormoran, as his dwelling-place, at the time when it was 'the White Rock in the Wood' and 6 miles inland. It is now an island at high tide. The giant needed a viewpoint high above the trees, and so he selected blocks of granite from the neighbouring hills and carried them here. His wife was given the task of carrying most of the blocks in her apron, and she wondered why it had to be granite and not any other kind of rock. There was a supply of greenstone rock close at hand, so when Cormoran was sleeping she broke some off and hurried towards the hill with it, hoping to put it in place before her husband awoke. But he saw what she was doing, and kicked her, so that her apron-string broke and the stone fell to the ground, where it now remains, known as Chapel Rock because in early Christian times a chapel was built upon it. The giant's wife was killed by a blow from a hammer being thrown by the giant who lived on Trecobben Hill – he and Cormoran shared the one hammer they possessed. The two giants lifted Chapel Rock and buried the giantess beneath it.

The Devil was also active in forming coastal landscape features, and some of them are named after him, such as the Devil's Bridge, a natural limestone arch on Worm's Head* (so called because of its serpent-like shape, 'worm' being an old name for a sea serpent), on the Gower peninsula (West Glamorgan). The Devil's Hole is a 100-foot-wide coastal crater on Jersey, where the movement of the sea causes eerie noises, and today there is a statue of the Devil beside the narrow path leading to his Hole. On Lundy Island, a chasm 370 feet deep and 250 feet wide is called the Devil's Limekiln after he blasted it out and dumped the rock offshore. The Devil's Frying Pan can be found just south of Cadgwith (Cornwall), a sea-cave with a collapsed roof. Filey Brig, a reef north of Filey (North Yorkshire), was also built by the Devil. He accidentally dropped his hammer into the sea, and made a grab for it with his sooty fingers. There happened to be a fish in the way, and as he touched it the Devil cried (for some reason best known to himself), 'Ah! Dick!' The fish has been called the haddock ever since, and also carries the mark of the Devil's fingers. Further north, at Newcastle (Tyne and Wear), the rocks known as the Black Middens were part of the Devil's plan to block up the River Tyne at its entrance. At a time when it looked as though the inhabitants of the city were becoming religious, he determined to cause trouble, and so started bringing apronsful of stones from Whitley quarry. On one such journey he was alarmed at meeting a woman, dropped his load, and fled. More misfortune attended his attempt to build a causeway across the sea to Lundy Island from the north Devon coast between Bucks Mills and Clovelly. He gave up when the handle of his shovel broke, leaving a rocky ridge which now extends about a quarter of a mile into the sea. On Shetland, the Holes of Scraada in Eshaness is a hole in the ground into which the sea flows through an underground channel 300 feet long.

This is said to have been carved out by the Devil as a punishment for wrecking ships on the Ve Skerries, though who handed down this punishment is not told.

It was Michael Scot, the northern magician, who ordered his three devils to build a causeway of sand to link Fortrose (Ross and Cromarty) with Ardersier (Inverness) on opposite sides of the Moray Firth. They worked under cover of darkness, and were making good progress until they were spotted just before dawn by a shepherd who was out early. He saw the new sandbar and the little men working on it, and in alarm he asked for God's blessing on it. This sent the devils packing, and they left the causeway unfinished before it could block the way for ships: today there is a sandspit projecting from each shore, but they do not meet. On the subject of sand, there are some fine sandy beaches around Britain's coast, but perhaps none so fine as the Sands of Luskentyre on Harris in the Outer Hebrides, which were once believed to be made of grains of pure gold. Anyone who was in need could come and fetch some, but one day a greedy man came with a pony and panniers and took away a load which he intended to carry over to the mainland in his boat and sell there. But his loaded boat was riding low in the sea, and a storm arose, swamping it so that it sank. Thus was the man punished for his greed, and in addition the sands were changed back to ordinary sand, only becoming gold again just as the sun is setting over the sea.

A familar penance in folklore is spinning ropes of sand, and one wrongdoer with this fate was Sir William Tracey, baron of Barnstaple and one of the murderers of Thomas à Becket. He is now said to haunt Crookham Cavern near Ilfracombe (Devon), where he is condemned to make bundles of sand. In another version, he is on Braunton Burrows near Barnstaple, spinning ropes of sand which are never finished, because a black dog with a ball of fire in its mouth comes and burns through the rope every time one nears completion. Jan or John Tregeagle, a real-life Cornish magistrate in the seventeenth century, had a bad reputation, and as a result his ghost was condemned to complete numerous impossible tasks, which included making sand ropes at Padstow, and sweeping Porthcurno Cove at Land's End clean of the sand which is washed in daily by the sea. A natural rock arch near Nare Head south of Falmouth was called Tregagle's Hole, and his voice is heard crying above the sound of a storm. He was also responsible for the formation of the sandbank called Loe Bar at Porthleven. He was clearing the beach at Berepper of sand and carrying it in sacks to Porthleven, an endless task because however much he carried away, the sea brought in more. One day he was tripped up by a demon, he dropped his sack of sand and it burst open, forming Loe Bar and closing the entrance to the harbour called the Loe, so that it became a lake. The Loe is one of the places where King Arthur is said to have been taken when he was at the point of death, and where he ordered Sir Bedivere to throw his sword Excalibur into the water. Other coastal sites for this legend are the Little Sea at Studland, and Poole Harbour (both in Dorset).

Sand dunes have also featured in legends as the place where a saint has arrived after journeying across the sea, usually in an unconventional way. In the fifth century St Piran came over to Cornwall from Ireland, from where he was forcibly expelled by being chained to a millstone and thrown off a cliff. The stormy weather instantly calmed, and he landed in the sea sitting on top of the millstone. He floated safely to Cornwall, landing on Penhale Sands* north of Perranporth. He built an oratory and hermitage there, but they were covered by sand in early medieval times, being rediscovered in the sixteenth and nineteenth centuries, and excavated. There is said to be a whole town buried under the dunes. Because of their evil ways, a storm blew up and the people and their dwellings were overwhelmed. On stormy nights the church bells can be heard above the howling wind. In Wales, the remains of a chapel in the sand dunes at Trearddur Bay on Anglesey (Gwynedd) mark the spot where St Ffraid (also known as Brigid) landed after sailing across the Irish Sea on a turf. An alternative landing site was near Conwy, where the turf attached itself to the coast. Elian was another saint who landed on Anglesey, after journeying from Rome. He came with all his goods and chattels and landed at Port Ychen (Port of the Oxen) near Llaneilian (where he then built his church). Proof of his landing is shown in the hoofmarks of his oxen on a rock by the shore.

The coastline of Britain is haunted by assorted ghosts and monsters, ranging from the evil spirits that can be heard screaming in rage or torment around the Farne Islands (Northumberland), after they were banished by St Cuthbert, to the fairy cattle of Skye, Tiree, Harris and Berneray in the Hebrides. These are similar to ordinary cattle, but hornless, and often dun in colour, or red and speckled. They will not graze on many land pastures, preferring to eat seaweed under the sea, where they usually live. Fairy dogs have also been seen on the Scottish islands. Their footprints have been found on the sand – 'as large as the spread of a [man's] palm' – and one man found two large puppies in the coastal cavern known as the Lair of the Faery Dog on Tiree, where the barking of a huge dog had been heard. Anyone finding evidence of a fairy dog's presence would quickly depart, because it was believed that if the dog overtook you, you would be destroyed. They were the size of a calf, dark green in colour, and they travelled silently in a straight line. They have much in common with the phantom black dogs which were commonly encountered in England and Wales, the green fairy dog being a purely Scottish creature. Black dogs haunted the Norfolk coastline in particular, where they were known as Black Shuck. Indeed, phantom black dogs are still seen today, and a coastguard saw one on the beach at Gorleston (Norfolk) in April 1972. It was running along the beach, and as he watched, it 'vanished before my eyes'. On the Isle of Portland (Dorset), the phantom dog was called a Row Dog (meaning rough, from his shaggy coat), and his main haunt was Cave Hole near Portland Bill. In stormy weather it was wise to keep out of his reach, because he was liable to come out of his hole and drag you into the sea, in the same way as the water spirits described in Chapter 2.

There were also believed to be kelpies in the sea, looking for victims as did the river kelpies in Chapter 2. Fishermen believed in a sea god to which they made offerings, perhaps of food, or of the first fish caught, and in Orkney and Shetland the fishermen would not save people from drowning, believing that the spirit of the waters must have his sacrifice. A kelpie which lived in the sea at St Bonne Nuit Bay, Jersey (Channel Islands), would agitate the water until boats could not ride the gigantic waves, and he would watch gleefully as they sank. The kelpies of the Minch (Outer Hebrides), and especially the channel separating Lewis from the Shiant Islands, took the form of blue men, and were known as the Blue Men of the Minch. They kept the water perpetually in turmoil, and lured ships to their doom. One man who claimed to have seen one of these kelpies described him as 'A blue-coloured man, with a long, grey face, and floating from the waist out of the water'. He followed the boat for a long time, and was sometimes so near that those in the boat could have touched him. According to legend, one was captured and bound with the strongest rope, but he was able to snap it easily, and leapt overboard to rejoin his companions. In the Scottish islands the Blue Men were believed to be fallen angels who were relegated to the sea, fairies being fallen angels relegated to the land. The kelpies of the Dornoch Firth on the eastern side of Scotland (Sutherland/Ross and Cromarty) used to cross the water in cockle-shells, and when they became tired of this they decided to build a bridge. But as in the tale of the causeway across the Moray Firth earlier in this chapter, a local man asked God to bless the bridge and its builders, and at the sound of God's name both bridge and workmen were covered by the tide. Today the whirlpool and quicksand known as the Gizzen Briggs at the entrance to the firth mark the place where the kelpies' bridge once briefly stood.

A Welsh water-horse was caught on the shore of Carmarthen Bay (Dyfed) by a man who led it home and tried to use it as a carthorse. But one day it took the cart and driver into the sea, and they were never seen again. The inhabitants of St Clement on Jersey (Channel Islands) once believed that a great bull with fiery eyes lived on the reefs of Les Grands Hommets, because his roaring could be heard at low tide. One brave man in a sand-eeling party on the reefs decided to track down the bull to its lair, and found that the roaring noise was caused by water from a rock pool pouring down a hole into the rock below, making a loud noise as it did so. Once the hole was blocked, the 'bull' was heard no more!

The Blue Men of the Minch was one group of non-human entities that sometimes appeared in human form in the sea around Britain, but there were also others appearing from time to time on the shore: ghosts, mermaids and fairies. The cliffs at Southwold (Suffolk) were haunted by a woman whose husband was drowned at sea. She had waited in vain for his return, but went mad and threw herself off the pier. When her ghost was seen, or heard shrieking, it was said that there was a gale blowing up. Storms were also predicted by the Whooper, named from the noise it made, which haunted Sennen Cove in Cornwall. A blanket of fog would come down to prevent the fishermen taking to sea when a storm was due. On the Isle of Man, a sea-cave called Black Head Creek was haunted by a group of fishermen. The story was that a pirate used the cave as a place to store his ill-gotten gains, and he left one of his crew in charge. He never returned, and in time the man left behind also disappeared. Then an old fisherman, who was working near the cave, saw a boat manned by six sailors in red caps who were rowing towards the cave mouth. They disappeared inside, and the old fisherman, curious to find out who they were, followed them. The cave, which only had one entrance, was empty. A Cornish cave called Willy Willcocks' Hole, in Chapel Cliff at Polperro, is haunted by the man who gave his name to the cave. He was a fisherman who got lost in the maze of tunnels inside the cave, and his ghost is still trying to find its way out. Also named from a ghost is a rock near Land's End (Cornwall). A boat from Ireland was ship-wrecked here, the only survivor being a woman who was seen sitting on top of the rock. Because of the storm, she couldn't be rescued, and after several days she died and was washed away by the sea. Afterwards, when the waves were high, fishermen would see her sitting on the rock, then known as the Irish Lady, with a rose in her mouth. Another woman who died a cruel death on the coast was Abigail Carstair, said to be a witch. She was chased over the edge of Whitestone Cliffs (North Yorkshire). Now the ghost of a monk dressed in white is said to patrol the clifftop to warn of the danger.

One of the strangest seaside tales, because it is supposed to be true, must be this one from the island of Muck in the Inner Hebrides. The events are said to have taken place in the early years of this century, and folklorist Alasdair Alpin MacGregor was told the story by the Revd Alexander Fraser, a minister in the islands, who was himself told it by an elder in his church. Two young brothers were on the shore looking for driftwood, and in a cove they found a tin which they decided to open. While they were hitting it with a stone, two tiny boys in green vests appeared and asked them in good English what they were doing. The green boys could also speak Gaelic, and asked the brothers about their home and family. A tiny boat was close by, with a tiny woman and a dog the size of a rat on board. The woman was also dressed in green, and invited the lads aboard for some tea. They wouldn't go to her, so she handed them a few tiny loaves of bread the size of a walnut, which they ate and enjoyed. Then the green boys said, 'We are departing now. When you see our boat out at the Dubh Sgeir [a black rock close to the shore], you must return home. We will not be coming back here any more; but others of our race will be coming.' Soon after the boat had left, the boys' sister found them gazing out to sea, and when she spoke to them her voice broke the spell. Although they had felt happy in the company of the little green people, they now felt frightened. Everybody was quite sure that they had met the fairies.

The Little People are believed to live in another world apart from ours, but into which there are entrances from our world. There are other non-human beings who live in an underwater world, and they are the mer-folk. There are numerous accounts of mermaids (and sometimes mermen) having been seen around the British coast, so let's start in Dyfed in south-west Wales where in July 1826 a family living on a farm at Llanuwchaiarn near Aberystwyth saw a mermaid perched on a stone close to the shore. She looked like a young woman, with short dark hair, a handsome face, and white skin, and there seemed to be something black, perhaps a tail, behind her. She appeared to be drinking water from her hand, and they heard her sneezing. The twelve members of the family watched her from the shore. Further south along the Dyfed coast, a mermaid was said to be often seen on a rock called Careg Ina near New Quay. One day she became entangled in fishermen's nets. She asked the men to release her, and in gratitude when they did so, she warned them that a storm was imminent, and they were able to get back to land before it struck. Others who were not warned, drowned. A fisherman near Pen Cemmaes took prisoner a mermaid he found doing her hair, but let her go when she pleaded with him, saying she would warn him 'in the time of thy greatest need'. Some time later, on a calm and hot afternoon, she rose up out of the sea and told him to take up his nets. The fisherman did so, and by the time he reached land, a violent storm had arisen, in which the other fishermen drowned. Another mermaid was captured at Llanwnda near Fishguard and kept hidden for some time, until she begged to be set free, giving her captors some advice including: 'Skim the surface of the pottage before adding sweet milk to it: it will be whiter and sweeter, and less of it will do.' She was clearly a culinary expert, though her advice means nothing to us today. Advice was also given by a mermaid seen by quarry workmen near Porth y Rhaw. This mermaid had flowing silvery hair and the body of a young girl, except that from the waist down she had a fish's body. She spoke in Welsh to the men, telling them: 'Reaping in Pembrokeshire and weeding in Carmarthenshire', words even more incomprehensible than the other's.

Moving south, Cornwall too has several mermaid legends, both Padstow and Seaton Sands (near Looe, and said to once have been a prosperous town) having had harbours overwhelmed by sand because of a mermaid's curse. At Seaton, sailors insulted her; at Padstow, someone shot at her while she was bathing. The singing of the mermaid who sat on Mermaid's Rock near Lamorna would foretell shipwreck, while the mermaid of Zennor appeared in the church in the guise of a human lady, and took away as husband one of the singers in the choir. Her portrait can still be seen on a bench-end in the church (*see plate 17*). Mermaids have also been seen at various places on the Dorset coast: at Church Ope Cove, Portland, where she came ashore, and sitting on Table Rock off Old Harry Point, Swanage. In Suffolk on the east coast, it is recorded that fishermen at Orford caught a strange wild man in their nets in 1511. He doesn't sound like the traditional merman, for he had a bald head, long beard, and hairy body. In captivity he was fed on raw flesh and fish, but never spoke to his captors. They allowed him to swim in the sea in a net, and he once escaped, but he returned to the castle where he was held captive. However he later escaped again, this time for good.

Scotland has many tales of mermaids, some clearly legendary, others possibly factual, such as the 1814 report of a merman seen off Port Gordon (Banffshire). In a letter dated 16 August and sent to the *Aberdeen Chronicle*, the Rathven schoolmaster George McKenzie described what happened to two fishermen. When returning to land one calm afternoon, they saw 'a creature of a tawny colour, appearing like a man sitting, with his body half-bent.' He had his back to them, and was half above the water. They quietly came closer, and when he heard them he turned and they saw his face. 'His countenance was swarthy, his hair short and curled, of a colour between a green and a grey: he had small eyes, a flat nose, his mouth was large, and his arms of an extraordinary length.' In the clear water they could see that from the waist down his body tapered. He suddenly dived, coming to the surface again nearby with what the fishermen thought was a female. Belief in the mermaid was widespread among seamen in the north-east of Scotland, and also in the Scottish Hebrides where there were many mermaid traditions. The Shetlands had their seal-folk, the Silkies or seals being thought able to turn into humans at will; the Orkneys had sea-trows, fairyfolk who could turn into seals. Of the many mermaid traditions, one final tale is of a mermaid who was buried on Benbecula some time in the last century. The mermaid was seen in the sea by men cutting seaweed, and a boy threw a stone at her. A few days later she was found lying dead on the rocks, and she was described as 'about the size of a well-fed child of three to four years with abnormally developed breasts. Hair long, dark and glossy; skin white, soft and tender. The lower part of the body like a salmon without scales.' Crowds of people came to see her, and a coffin and shroud were made for her, and she was buried near the shore. If the grave could now be located, and the burial disinterred, would a post-mortem be able to confirm the existence of mermaids?

Pools and Lakes

Large areas of water are naturally mysterious places: because you can't see the bottom of a lake, you can imagine that it might be bottomless; because its interior is hidden, you can imagine that the water covers a drowned town, or that there might be treasure lying there, or fairies living there, or a mermaid, or a water monster; because someone has drowned there, you can imagine that a water-spirit demands sacrifices. A wide variety of folklore has grown up around pools and lakes, a sample of which we will review here.

Formation legends usually focus on the arrival of the water rather than the depression in which the water lies, but a story from Shetland does explain how the depression was made. A giant who lived in a range of hills called the Kaems was tormented by trows (trolls) who would climb over him, into his ears, and pull his eyebrows. He decided to carry them over to Norway in a basket, and when he had finished making a basket of straw, he went and scooped up all the trows one moonlit night. But once they were fastened inside, he couldn't easily lift the basket; and when he succeeded, the bottom collapsed, the trows tumbled out, and the giant overbalanced. He came down on one knee, which left a gap in the hills, and his foot made a gash in the earth, which eventually filled up with water and became Pettawater. It is said that the marks of his toes can still be seen. No one knows where the giant went after that, but the trows still dance around the lake.

Overflowing springs were sometimes said to be the reason that a valley became filled with water. The Cailleach Bheur was a Highland hag, possibly the memory of a pagan goddess, who was responsible for the formation of Loch Awe (Argyll). In one version her foot struck an obstacle, perhaps intentionally, thus releasing all the underground springs that began to flow into the valley. In another version, she was in charge of a well on the mountain called Ben Cruachan, where she pastured her goats, and she had to place a stone over the well at sunset to stop its flow, and remove it at sunrise. One evening she fell asleep and so forgot to cover the well, with the result that when she awoke she found the valley below full of water, having covered fertile farm-land and drowned men and animals. In horror at what had happened, she turned into stone. Another Highland lake formed from a well overflow was Loch Ness* (Inverness). When the valley was a fertile plain, anyone using a spring in the middle of the valley had to replace its covering stone immediately after use, but one woman who was drawing water heard her child scream and she ran to it, forgetting to cover the well. The water overflowed and filled the valley, causing the people to cry as they fled to the hills: 'Tha loch nis ann' (There is a loch there now) – hence the name Loch Ness.

Several Welsh lakes also formed when wells were left uncovered, such as Llyn Llech Owen (Dyfed) near Gorslas, where there are several versions of the story: a boy who daily watered a farmer's horse at the well one day forgot to put back the stone afterwards; or it was a man named Owen who watered his horse, and when he found that the water was overflowing because he had forgotten to put the stone back, he rode round the flood as fast as he could, with the aim of stopping it from drowning the whole valley – hence the lake was called The Lake of Owen's

Flagstone (Llyn Llech Owen). The name 'Owen' may refer either to the hero Owen Glendower, or another Welsh hero Owen Lawgoch.

In North Wales Ffynnon Grassi (Grace's Well) near Llangybi (Gwynedd) was also supposed to be kept covered except when water was being drawn, but someone left it open, and the resulting lake is now called Glasfryn. Grace may have been the well's guardian, but whoever she was, she was often seen wandering up and down the field called Cae'r Ladi (Lady's Field), moaning and weeping. She was also said to haunt the nearby house of Glasfryn, and witnesses in the nineteenth century saw a tall lady dressed in white silk and with a white velvet bonnet. A standing stone in the field above the well and the lake looks from certain angles like a woman hurrying along, and as late as the last century the stone would be whitewashed and decorated with an old bonnet and shawl (*see plate 18*). Also in Gwynedd, Bala Lake* was again said to have been formed when a well opposite Llangower (a village now on the lakeside) was inadvertently left uncovered one night. By morning there was a lake 3 miles long in the valley, and the old town of Bala lay beneath it. But in another version, the town was drowned because of a prince's cruelty. He would occasionally hear a voice crying 'Vengeance, vengeance', but would ignore it. One night, a harper playing at a celebration in the palace heard the voice, and saw a bird hovering above him, beckoning to him to follow. He followed it up into the hills, where he rested. When next morning he looked down at the town, he saw only a lake, and the harp that he had left behind was floating on the water.

Other Welsh lakes, and some in England, are said to conceal drowned settlements, though sometimes the prophecy has not yet come true, as is the case at Welshpool (Powys) where Llyn Du, between the town and Powis Castle, will one day engulf the town. Llangorse Lake* (also called Llyn Safaddan, Brecknock Mere, Talyllyn Pool and Lake of Brycheiniog) not far from Brecon (Powys) conceals a city drowned either because of the sinful lifestyle of its inhabitants, or in revenge for a murder. In Gwent, the Pool of Avarice near Cwmbran was said to be the

89

tomb of a big house and its occupants, who refused help to a relative who had fallen on hard times. As he departed after his unsuccessful request, the mountain crashed down on the house, and a pool filled the crater it made. Kenfig Pool* north of Porthcawl (Mid Glamorgan) is said to hold the drowned town of Kenfig, and there may be something in this belief, because traces of buildings are sometimes found in the surrounding sand dunes. The theme of vengeance also features in the story told to explain the inundation, as at Bala, though this time in revenge for a murder. Crymlyn Lake not far away allegedly covers the old town of Swansea, while Llyn-y-Maes at Treflyn (Dyfed) covers the original Tregaron. The wicked inhabitants were warned that if they did not improve their behaviour and cease their orgies and incessant revelry, their dwellings would be destroyed by fire and flood. They took no notice, and one night lightning set fire to the place, and a flood inundated it. Not far away, Pencarreg Lake near Llanybyther conceals a village, and is also said to be bottomless (so what does the village rest on?), while Talley Lakes by Talley Abbey, also in Dyfed, are likewise the site of a former town.

In England, lakes with drowned villages include Bomere (just south of Shrewsbury, where the people were drowned for their wickedness, despite being warned by the priest), the mere at Ellesmere* (where a well overflowed to drown the people who owned it, in punishment for charging too much for the water), and Llynclys Pool near Oswestry (which holds a drowned palace, about which a story similar to that of Bala Lake is told, even with the harpist and floating harp). These last three pools are in Shropshire, and numerous other lakes have similar traditions. They may have developed from memories of the lake-dwellings that were built and occupied in prehistoric times.

Some pools are said to have swallowed up individual people, and vehicles. At the foot of Duddle Hill north-east of Dorchester (Dorset) is Heedless William's Pond, which got its name from a coachman whose driving was somewhat hectic. One night he drove a coach and four into the pond, drowning himself and his passengers. All that remained visible above the surface was his whip-stick, still in its socket: after a while it came into bud, took root, and turned into a tree. In another version, it was a drunken mail van driver who ran his vehicle into the pond. Hell Kettles, three small ponds between Darlington and Croft (Durham), swallowed up a farmer who insisted on carting hay on St Barnabas's Day, together with his cart and horses, and they can still be seen through the clear water, according to the story. The Picktree Brag, a shape-shifting goblin who haunted the village of Picktree near Pelton (Durham), was in the habit of changing into a horse or donkey, tempting people to climb on his back, and then throwing them into a certain pond at a crossroads, himself sometimes disappearing into the water also. This behaviour resembles that of the Scottish kelpie we met in Chapter 2, with its overtones of sacrificial victims, and indeed pools and lakes sometimes house water-spirits that seek victims. Loch Wan (that is, Lamb's Loch) in Aberdeen/Banff claimed the sacrifice of the first lamb of the flock from each of the tenants grazing the land round about, and any tenant omitting to make this offering would find that half his sheep had drowned during the season.

The spirit of Llyn Gwernan south-west of Dolgellau (Gwynedd) took the form of a green man who watched people climbing Cadair Idris and when they were high up this mountain he would shout 'The hour is come! The hour is come!' and bring down mists, low cloud and storms, so that the people got lost and fell over the cliffs. He would then take all the bodies back to his home in the lake. In another version, a voice was heard calling from the water, 'The hour is come but the man is not!' The man who heard this, then saw an insane-looking man wearing only a shirt running towards the lake, and he stopped him from jumping in. The same cry was said to have been heard at Llyn Cynwch* north of Dolgellau (Gwynedd). The spirit of Lochan-nan-deaan between Corgarff and Tomintoul (Aberdeen/Banff) also demanded human sacrifice, and many had died there. The spirit sometimes took human form, as for example when some men decided to take water from the lake. Just as they were about to begin, they heard a terrific cry from the water and a little man wearing a red cap appeared. As the men fled, he roared loudly, and then vanished into the water. This story demonstrates that the spirit was protective of his lake, and in a similar way the Fuath was a spirit on South Uist (Outer Hebrides) who protected the fish in the lochs and rivers. Anyone who went fishing at spawning time was at risk. One man saw something like a mill wheel coming down the hill, and he fled leaving his fish behind. When he returned for them the next day, they had gone. Another man catching spawning fish met the Fuath in the form of a huge black man who threw him into a river pool.

Some pools and lakes were believed to conceal fairy dwellings. A man fell into Llyn Cynwch* near Dolgellau (Gwynedd) and was welcomed by the inhabitants who lived at the bottom, staying with them for about a month. The fairies had a garden on an invisible island in Llyn Cwm Llwch in the Brecon Beacons (Powys). On May Day a door would open in a rock by the lake. It led into a cave, and thence under the lake to the island. One man who visited the island took a flower back with him, and the door never opened again. As with Lochan-nan-deaan described above, when some men tried to cut through the dam holding the water in the lake, in order to drain it, the spirit of the lake, in the form of a man in a red coat, or a giant, or an old woman, appeared and warned that if they continued, enough water to drown Brecon would be released. Even if it is not specifically stated, the existence of Fairyland at or in a pool or lake is suggested by fairy activity there. The Little People were believed to frequent Llyn Tarw near Carno (Powys), and as recently as 1936 a mother and her children heard the sweetest singing there, though they could not see where the sound was coming from. Local farmers said that they too had heard it, and the tradition went back years. A man fishing in Llyn Cwmsilin south of Nantlle (Gwynedd) listened to music such as he had never heard before and watched a group of men about a foot tall dancing and leaping, but when he went too near to them they threw dust into his eyes and disappeared while he was trying to clear his vision. The fairies of Crymlyn Lake near Briton Ferry (West Glamorgan) were people turned into fairies by St Patrick. On a visit from Ireland to see St David, the people had insulted him, so he changed them into fishes, and some of the women into fairies. A kind fairy who helped an Anglesey (Gwynedd) woman by bringing her a loaf of bread weekly in return for the loan of her gridiron for bread-baking, always told the woman not to look when she left the house. But one day the woman did look, and saw the fairy go straight to Llyn Rhosddu which was near the house at Newborough, and plunge into the water. She never saw the fairy again. The fairies were industrious, not always singing and dancing, and in Scotland they had a dyeing factory beside a pool in Green Hollow, itself between Ben Ime and Ben Vane (Dunbarton/Argyll). The seclusion of the place was a great advantage, but their human neighbours kept trying to watch them at work, and one day when lookouts reported some men coming up to the hollow, the fairies, having no time to hide their equipment, decided to abandon it in the pool, which explains why the water of the pool in Green Hollow is now a vivid green colour.

There are some tales of human men having married fairy women from lake dwellings. The bottomless pool of Corwrion near Bethesda (Gwynedd) hid a fairy dwelling, though sometimes the fairies would be seen mowing hay on the lake shore, and their cattle would graze in the fields. The fairies' singing was also heard, and they were seen dancing gracefully. They helped their human neighbours, and tried to teach them to keep all their promises. A man whose wife was helping him to plough, treated her harshly, thus breaking his pledge to her, and no sooner had he done this, than he was pulled through the air and plunged into the lake. When his wife went to the lake to ask for him back, she was told that he was there, and there he should be. A young man fell in love with one of the fairies he saw dancing, and eventually they were married, but he had to agree to certain terms: he could not know her real name, but could call her whatever he wished; and if ever she misbehaved he might beat her with a rod, but he must never strike her with iron, for she would then leave him at once. After they had been married for some years, they went out to the fields to catch a pony, and the husband meant to throw his wife a halter, but instead he threw a bridle with an iron bit, which struck her. Immediately she flew through the air and plunged head-first into Corwrion Pool. She never returned to him, but once she came back to their bedroom window and gave him some instructions concerning their children. Numerous other stories about the fairies of Corwrion were once current, and it was also believed that the pool concealed a drowned town.

A young man who watched his family's cattle grazing by Llyn-y-Fan-Fach in the Black Mountains (Dyfed) saw a beautiful woman sitting on the water and combing her hair. He offered her bread and cheese, which she refused, and on the following day she again refused. On the third day she accepted his bread, and they became man and wife. She agreed to live with him until he should give her three blows without cause, and brought with her a large quantity of sheep, cattle, goats and horses. They lived happily on a farm and had three sons, but over the years the husband sometimes forgot the agreement, and on three occasions gave his wife a light slap or blow, though never in anger. She did not want to leave, because she loved her husband and they had been happy together, but she had to. She gathered together her cattle and went back to the lake. Her sons would often go there to look for her, and one day she came out to them. She gave the eldest a bag of medical prescriptions and instructions and told them that their work was to heal the sick. On other occasions she instructed them in the medicinal uses of herbs growing on the mountain. They wrote down this knowledge, and became known as the Physicians of Myddfai. Their descendants were still practising medicine in the area during the eighteenth century.

A similar story, but without the detail of the sons becoming famous physicians, was told about Llyn y Forwyn in the Rhondda (Mid Glamorgan), and this fairy likewise, when returning to the lake after three quarrels, also took her cattle with her. Fairy cows often feature in Welsh fairy tales. A farmer found a calf in the rushes beside Llyn Arennig, near Bala (Gwynedd), and took it home, where in time it produced many fine cattle. One summer's day, a little man came by, playing a pipe and calling the cattle by name:

Mulican, Molican, Malen, Mair,
Dowch adre rwan ar fy ngair.
(Come home now at my command.)

At which they all followed him into the lake and were never seen again. The cattle which went into Llyn y Forwyn, and Llyn y Fan Fach, were also named, and their names included Milfach, Malfach, Ali, Melen, Joco, Tegwen, Cornwen.

The fairy cows which grazed around Llyn Barfog near Aberdovey (Gwynedd) were milk-white, and one of them strayed into a farmer's herd. It was a fine producer of milk, butter, cheese, and calves, and when it grew old he decided to fatten it up for the butcher. In due time, when the butcher was raising his axe to slaughter it, a loud cry was heard, and the assembled people saw one of the ladies of the lake, dressed in green, standing on a crag above the lake, arms raised, and calling her stray cow home. It immediately went to her, together with its offspring and their offspring, and they all disappeared into the water. At Llyn dau Ychain (the Lake of the Two Oxen) near Cerrigydrudion (Clwyd) the cow that entered the water, accompanied by her offspring, two long-horned oxen, was the Freckled Cow that had lived on the Denbigh Moors, giving milk to all who needed it. She could never be milked dry – until a wicked hag milked her into a sieve. The Freckled Cow disappeared after this ill-treatment, tradition telling that she went into the lake. It was by this same lake that a harper, walking home late one night after playing for a party, came across a palace with lights blazing. A footman invited him inside, and he found a grand ball in full swing. He was asked to play his harp, which he did, and the company filled his hat with gold and silver. As dawn approached, the guests left one by one, until only the harper was left. He lay down to sleep on a magnificent couch – but when he awoke at midday, the couch had become a pile of heather, the palace had vanished, and the gold and silver was only dead leaves.

The harper lost his treasure, but some lakes are said to conceal hidden treasure, and that in Loch Stack (Sutherland) was said to be a Viking hoard of gold hidden by its owner, and now guarded by a black fairy dog which lives in the loch. The treasure in Grisedale Tarn (Cumbria) takes the form of King Dunmail's crown, while the bottomless Sowley Pond near Lymington (Hampshire) allegedly contains a life-size gold statue placed there by the monks of Beaulieu Abbey. In Northumberland, a pool called the Whirl Dub (in Whittle Dene, Nafferton) was believed to conceal Lord Lonkin's treasure wrapped in a hide. A man who used cart-horses to try and drag it out, shouted 'Pull, horses, pull, whether God will or not!', and thereby lost it again.

Similar events sometimes feature in attempts to lift church bells which are sunk in a pool or river, as we have already seen in Chapter 2 when an attempt was being made to raise Marden church bell in Herefordshire. In Shropshire, bells from a chapel which was said to once stand by the lake, are heard ringing in Colemere* near Ellesmere, and an attempt was once made to retrieve the bells, which had been thrown into the water by Oliver Cromwell's men. Chains were fastened to them, and twenty oxen were used to drag them to the side. They were almost out, when one of the men helping said, 'In spite of God and the Devil we have done it!' Whereupon the chains snapped and the bells rolled back into the water, never to be seen or heard again. In Cheshire, a bell from Rostherne church fell into Rostherne Mere when the bells were being hung. It was almost saved from sinking into the water, but on the third attempt to catch it before it sank, a workman cursed it, and it sank to the bottom where it has stayed. It is rung from time to time by the mermaid who is said to live in the mere, but we will meet her again later in this chapter. There is also, according to legend, a bell in Combermere (Cheshire), which fell overboard when bells from the abbey were being taken across the water to Wrenbury church. When it fell, the man in charge cursed it, whereupon he disappeared overboard with the bell. In one version of the story, the spirit of the water in the form of a demon came out of the mere and dragged him below.

One of the best-known stories from the Arthurian legends is the incident at the end of Arthur's life when, after he had been mortally wounded in battle, he ordered his knight Sir Bedivere to throw away his famous sword Excalibur. This had been given to Arthur by the Lady of the Lake, and now he wanted it returned to her, so Bedivere threw it into the lake and a hand came out, grasped the sword, and took it under. There are numerous contenders claiming to be the lake where this happened. Apart from the mere at Pomparles Bridge, Glastonbury (Somerset), which of course is not very far away from King Arthur's Grave at Glastonbury Abbey, one of the best known contenders is in Cornwall: Dozmary Pool* on Bodmin Moor; while another contender in England is Broomlee Lough in Northumberland. (This lake also contains treasure which cannot be pulled out.) In Wales, Excalibur may be hidden in a lake at Bosherston (Dyfed), or in Llyn Llydaw on the east side of Snowdon (Gwynedd). Another lake linked to the King Arthur story was Tarn Wadling (at High Hesket, Cumbria, but drained in the last century), where King Arthur had to solve a riddle which resulted in Sir Gawain offering to marry a hag, who then turned into a beautiful woman.

Some lakes are haunted by hags, others by ghostly white ladies, and yet others by the Devil himself. One of his homes was said to be in Loch Guinach near Kingussie (Inverness), where he spent several months each year, and when he came out of the water in the spring he made a wave which often flooded the nests of the black-headed gulls living on the edge of the loch. But this pleased him, because the gulls were thought to be the messengers of the angels, and to contain the spirits of people who performed good deeds while alive and who will eventually become angels themselves. Another Scottish haunt of the Devil's was Loch Shin (Sutherland) where he was accustomed to fish. A couple walking by the loch saw a man fishing from a stone, accompanied by a yellow dog, and they asked him if he would give them some trout for their supper. No sooner had they spoken than the angler flared up in a great fireball which rolled towards them, sending them running for their lives. Loch Achilty in Ross and Cromarty (west of Strathpeffer) was one of the places where the Devil would take a bath, and after he had spent the night wallowing in the suds, the water was very hot.

His soap left the lake covered with dirty suds, but they were eventually replaced by a carpet of white water-lilies. One of his haunts in England was Halls Garden Pond at Albury (Hertfordshire), which may also contain one of the church bells. Other pools contain spirits which have been banished there, such as Cranmere Pool on Dartmoor (Devon), where the ghost of the Okehampton merchant Benjamin Gayer, 'Binjy', was imprisoned, doomed to spin ropes of sand, or empty the pool with a thimble with a hole in it. In Cornwall, the evil magistrate Jan Tregeagle was doomed to empty Dozmary Pool* with a leaking limpet shell.

Ghosts and spirits haunt a number of pools and lakes, some of the ghosts even being those of inanimate objects, such as the ghostly lugger (a working boat) once said to haunt Croft Pasco Pool on Goonhilly Downs (Cornwall), and the ghostly pony and trap said to rush along the Beccles road at Gorleston (Norfolk) and plunge into the water-filled 'Lily Pit'. On the road between Scawby and Broughton (Humberside), it was said that a man once followed a phantom coach and horses into a lake, and was drowned. On dark nights the coachman can sometimes be heard laughing. A few lake ghosts are male – Loch Ness* (Inverness) was said to have a ghost called the Old Man of Inverfarigaig, seen in the lakeside trees, or heard shrieking during winter storms; and the phantom skater of Hickling Broad (Norfolk) was a drummer boy who used to skate across the ice to meet his sweetheart in secret, until the day he fell through and was drowned, his ghost afterwards retracing his steps. But ghosts seen at pools and lakes are usually female, and often dressed in white. From a deep ('bottomless') water-filled pit in Morton parish near Gainsborough (Lincolnshire), a lady in white was said to rise at midnight, and travel over the surrounding countryside; while the White Lady of Hell-Clough rose from a pool at Norton, Sheffield (South Yorkshire), and floated across a field and into a wood. The White Lady of Longnor came out of the 'bottomless' Black Pool beside the road to Leebotwood (Shropshire) and wandered the lanes. A young man who saw her some time during the last century thought she was a living girl and decided to give her a fright: 'I waited till 'er come close up to me, right i' the middle o' the bridge, an' I stretched out my arms . . . an' I clasped 'er in 'em, tight . . . An' theer was nothin'!' She was believed to be the ghost of a lady who had been 'disappointed', and so had drowned herself in the pool.

A nun dressed in white is believed to haunt Wepre Pool at Connah's Quay (Clwyd), seen there in recent years by anglers. The story to explain her presence is that she found an abandoned baby on the convent doorstep and took it to the nearby Wepre Brook to wash it, but it fell into the water and drowned. This so upset the nun that she later returned to the brook and drowned herself. As in this case, the people who haunt pools and lakes are often said to have died tragically there. Another such death was that of Kitty, an old woman who drowned in the pool now known as Kit's Steps at Lydford Gorge* (Devon), her ghost sometimes being seen there. But hauntings sometimes foreshadow death for the witnesses. In another tale from Clwyd, a couple heard the sounds of a ghostly battle while passing a lake called Chwythlyn near Llangernyw, during the autumn of 1891. They had become lost in fog which had suddenly come down, and for more than an hour they heard the sounds of a battle being fought all around them. Then the fog lifted and they were alone in a wood by the lake. Some months later, their bodies were found floating in the lake, but no one ever discovered how they came to be there.

Again in Clwyd, this time during the winter of 1852, a farm labourer called John Roberts came into contact with the spirits of Pwll-y-Wrach (The Hag's Pool) on Flint Mountain, an encounter that foretold his death. One day when leaving home for his work, he found a strange youth blocking his door. As he went to push him away, he felt himself hurtling through the air, and found himself in the mud beside Pwll-y-Wrach with a weight upon him. Only at dawn when he heard the cock crow was he released, to find the youth standing over him, and the youth said, 'When the cuckoo sings its first note at Flint Mountain, I shall come again to fetch you.' In the following May, a wall fell on John Roberts and killed him: a witness said that she had seen a cuckoo perch in a tree at the time of his death, and this same cuckoo then followed the body, singing, when it was carried home.

Other pools and lakes are believed to predict deaths, for example whenever an heir of the Brereton family was about to die, tree trunks would be seen floating on the surface of Bagmere (Cheshire); while Bathe Pool, North Tawton (Devon), would overflow before the death of a member of the Royal Family, or before a war. Garendon Pool near Loughborough (Leicestershire) turned red like a pool of blood during 1645, the year of the Battle of Naseby, and this was believed to be a sign from God of his anger at the Civil War. Then the 'blood' cleared, and this was seen as a sign that the war would soon end. In Hampshire, Ocknell Pond in the New Forest (Hampshire), close to the Rufus Stone, is said to turn red every August because it was here that Walter Tirel, the murderer of William Rufus, king of England, washed his hands after the murder. The spirit of Loch Ussie, between Dingwall and Strathpeffer (Ross and Cromarty), is said to answer questions about the future. The questioner must ask his or her question out loud, and the answer is 'Yes' if the question is followed by a silence, or 'No' if groaning or snarling are heard or ripples seen on the water. The lake also has links with the Brahan Seer, a famous Scottish prophet, who was born near here around 1600. One story tells that the seer's stone, which had a hole through which he looked to see into the future, was hidden in the loch, which explains its powers of prophecy. Any attempt to try and find the stone would result in the loch overflowing and drowning Strathpeffer. Loch Ussie is seen as an eerie place where no fish will live, which birds will not fly over, and where the voices of people crying out in distress can be heard after dark.

As with Loch Ussie, birds flying over Llyn Moel Llyn, in Llanfihangel Genau'r Glyn (Dyfed), were said to fall dead into the water; and it was also said of this lake that any attempt to drain it would be followed by terrific thunderstorms. When workmen began to drain Harbottle Lough (Northumberland) a voice was heard in the water, saying 'Let alone; let alone!' and threatening to drown the places round about if the work was continued. A voice was heard from Lake Bala* (Gwynedd) when an attempt was made to find its depth. It cried: 'Line cannot fathom me. Go, or I will swallow you up!' If Llyn Eiddwen (Dyfed) ever dries up, it was believed that the town of Carmarthen will sink.

Unexpectedly, for they are usually thought of as sea-going creatures, mermaids are said to live in several pools and lakes. The folklore surrounding them contains themes we have already encountered in this chapter. The mermaid of Aqualate Mere (Staffordshire) would appear when a calamity was due. She originally lived in Newport Mere (Shropshire) not far away but left when the water dried up. She also warned what would happen if her new home were to dry up, putting her head out of the water on one occasion when workmen were doing some dredging work and saying to them: 'If this mere you do let dry, Newport and Meretown I will destr'y.' Similarly, the mermaid of Blake Mere (also known as Black Mere, or the Mermaid's Pool) at Morridge near Leek (Staffordshire) warned workmen that if the water was let out, Leek would be drowned. There was another Mermaid's Pool on Kinder Scout (Derbyshire): she would appear at dawn on Easter Day, and anyone seeing her would live for ever. Needless to say, neither ever happened. The mermaid in Rostherne Mere (Cheshire) was also believed to appear at Easter's dawn. She was rarely seen, however, preferring to sit on a church bell at the bottom of the mere. Sometimes she would ring the bell, and sometimes she would sing. Equally shy was the mermaid of Llyn Fawr in the Rhondda valley (Mid Glamorgan). She had a fish-like lower body, and would sit combing her long golden hair, but if anyone came by, she would dive into the water. She sounds like the fairy women who lived in the lakes and sometimes married human men. Similarly, a group of maidens who drowned in Llyn y Morynion near Ffestiniog (Gwynedd) resemble both mermaids and fairy women. They were women fetched from the Vale of Clwyd to be wives for some young men from Ardudwy, but the men were attacked and killed on the way back home. The maidens leapt into the lake and drowned themselves in response to this tragedy, and were afterwards seen on the lake shore early in the morning, combing their hair.

The mermaid of Loch Benachally near Lornty (Perthshire) had unfriendly intentions: she tried to entice a laird who was passing on his horse, by pretending she was drowning. Had he not been grabbed by his manservant, she would have taken him into the water. In this behaviour she resembles the kelpie, who as we saw in Chapter 2 was always on the lookout to capture and kill unwary humans by taking the form of a horse or a human being and trying to entice them into the water. Kelpies lived in pools and lakes in Scotland as well as in rivers. Two men fishing in Loch Borralan (Sutherland) saw the water-horse but unwisely didn't flee: they were never seen again, and all that was found was their rods, the fish they had caught, and the hoof-prints of a huge horse. The Loch Garve* (Ross and Cromarty) water-horse lives in a house under the surface, and the heat from its chimney keeps that part of the lake unfrozen in winter. People bathing in Loch Pityoulish near Aviemore (Inverness) would take care not to submerge their heads, for fear of being pulled under by the black water-horse that lived there in a sunken prehistoric lake-dwelling. One day, so it was said, the heir to the Barony of Kincardine and some young friends were playing on the lake shore when they saw a beautiful horse grazing close by. It had a silver harness, saddle and reins, and they grabbed at the reins, whereupon the horse dragged them into the lake, their fingers stuck like glue to the reins. The only one who survived was the heir: he severed his fingers with a knife he carried with him.

Water-bulls lived in some Scottish lochs, but they were comparatively harmless. They were rarely seen, but sometimes were spotted grazing with ordinary cattle. The monster of Loch Garten (Inverness) was visually a cross between a horse and a bull, and its loud roars were heard at night. It was dangerous because it preyed on lambs and children, so one man decided to try and get rid of it. He baited a gaff with a lamb, and led a rope from the gaff to a huge boulder on the loch shore. He tied the rope round the boulder, then rowed into the loch and threw the gaff with its lamb overboard. He then went home. During the night a tremendous storm raged, and people heard the roars of the monster above the noise of the thunder. Next morning, the boulder had gone from the loch shore, a deep rut leading into the water showing that the monster had dragged it in when he took the bait. He was never seen again. Another noisy monster was the one that was believed to live in Loch Awe (Argyll), which was said to have twelve legs and was like a great horse, or a giant eel, and was heard rather than seen. When the loch became frozen over, it could be heard breaking up the ice.

People really did believe that water-horses, water-bulls and other monsters lived in the lakes, because from time to time they saw them. In 1857 Lord Malmesbury wrote in his *Memoirs:*

> My stalker, John Stuart at Achnacarry, has seen it twice, and both times at sunrise in summer, when there was not a ripple on the water. The creature was basking on the surface; he saw only the head and hind-quarters, proving that its back was hollow, which is not the shape of any fish, or of a seal. Its head resembled that of a horse. The Highlanders are very superstitious about this creature. They believe that there is never more than one in existence at the same time.

The lake he was writing about was Loch Arkaig (Inverness). Only a few years later, the people who lived near Loch nan Dubhrachan in the Sleat of Skye were actually trying to capture a water-horse by dragging the loch. They were afraid to pass the loch at night, when the beast would lie in wait for them, so in 1870 a large net was used to drag the loch. When the net became entangled with something under the water, the workmen and the watchers became so frightened that they ran for their homes. It is possible that the water-horse they were trying to capture may not have been simply a creation of folklore, but a real monster. There are still today persistent reports of monsters being seen in numerous Scottish lochs, most notably of course Loch Ness* (Inverness). The most determined efforts of sceptical scientists to kill off Nessie (as the monster is affectionately known) have not yet succeeded. Other lochs where monsters have reportedly been seen in recent years include Eil, Shiel (in Moidart), Lochy,

Oich and Morar (all in Inverness). Perhaps some of the other monsters believed to live in the lochs, such as the kelpie, were once based on reality, rather than being totally legendary.

Monsters of the sort believed to live in the Inverness lochs are rarely reported from the lakes of England, though occasionally something will be seen in a Welsh lake, such as Bala* (Gwynedd), where a monster has been sighted in recent years. None of the first-hand reports of lake monsters has ever described the creature as harming humans, so the story of Llyn-y-Gadair near Cadair Idris (Gwynedd) is likely to be fictional. It tells how, in the eighteenth century, a man swam across the lake, followed by a long object. His friends went to meet him as he reached the shore, but at that point the monster raised its head and wrapped the man in its coils, taking him to a deep part of the lake and leaving blood-stained water in its wake.

A watery environment was sometimes used by a dragon as its hideaway, like the Dragon of Aller which lived in the bogs of Sedgemoor, or the Athelney fens, only coming out to terrorize the neighbourhood. It was eventually slain with a spear, and one said to be the same weapon is still on show in Low Ham church (Somerset). A deep pool known as the Knucker Hole, near Lyminster church (West Sussex) was once the home of the Lyminster Knucker, another dragon which made a nuisance of itself by eating men and cattle. The name Knucker comes from the Old English *nicor*, used in the eighth-century poem *Beowulf* to describe a water-monster. Although these monsters have been given fanciful descriptions and behaviour in folktales, the fact that people still report seeing water-monsters today, both in lakes and in the sea, and in many parts of the world, strongly suggests that at least some of the folktales that amuse us today were originally based on fact.

Rocks and Stones

Just as the activities of giants and the Devil were responsible for the shapes of hills and mountains, as described in Chapter 1, so also do many large rocks and stones scattered across the countryside mark the former presence of these superbeings. Stones might be pebbles thrown from his shoes by a giant, as with the Stones of Aled, two boulders of many tons in weight which lie on the slopes of Moel y Gaseg Wen, a hill near Llansannan (Clwyd). Three large rocks at the foot of Cadair Idris (Gwynedd) were three pebbles (or grains of sand) shaken from his shoes by the giant Idris before climbing to his chair on top of the mountain. While the Devil was sitting in his chair on the Stiperstones* (Shropshire) one day, he pulled a pebble from his shoe and threw it 5 miles to Bishop's Castle, where it landed near the now-ruined castle and became known as the Lea Stone. A boulder in the bed of the River Sawdde in the Black Mountains (Powys) was a stone from the shoe of one of King Arthur's lady friends, while another beside it was a quoit thrown by the king from the summit of Pen Arthur a mile away. Two stones several tons in weight that used to stand in front of

Bromsgrove Town Hall (Worcestershire) (buried in 1806 because too big to move when the road was paved) were shaken from the shoes of Sir Ryalas Bolton, the 'Jovial Hunter' who allegedly slew the wild boar which lived in Boar's Grove, from which the name of Bromsgrove was said to have derived. Alternatively, the Jovial Hunter had a rival who lived at Malvern and they threw stones at each other, which collided and fell to earth at Bromsgrove.

If folktales are any guide, it would seem that the superbeings spent a lot of their time throwing missiles at each other and at their enemies. Their aim was often faulty, and a giant who lived on a hill near Edderton (Ross and Cromarty) and wanted to throw a rock at a rival above Tain, failed to hit him because he had been feasting and drinking the previous night and was lacking in strength. His missile fell short, landing at Glenmorangie. The giants of many other Scottish counties were also keen on throwing rocks about. The strongest Scottish giant was called Samson, and he lived on Ben Ledi near Callander (Perth). He challenged all the Scottish giants to a trial of strength at 'putting the stone', and was the winner. Samson's Putting Stone is a large boulder on the lower eastern slope of the Ben. Another giant called Samson lived in a cave at Enville (Staffordshire). He was caught kissing the wife of a giant who lived at Holy Austin Rock. Enraged, the latter picked up a stone shaped like a javelin and threw it after the fleeing Samson. It landed on its sharp end and stuck into the ground, being afterwards known as the Bolt Stone.

On the Isle of Man, Goddard Crovan's Stone was also thrown because of a woman, but this time it was thrown at the woman, and in fact it killed her. Goddard Crovan lived with his wife in a castle on top of Barrule, but he could not stand the sound of her voice constantly berating him, so he turned her out. As she went down the mountain, and feeling herself beyond his reach, she turned and started shouting at him again, so he picked up this 20–30 ton granite boulder and hurled it after her. (Many a hen-pecked husband will no doubt feel in sympathy with Goddard Crovan!) A giant who was ravaging the Dorset countryside

nearly got his comeuppance from the villagers of Brockhampton Green, who earmarked a large stone with which to kill him. But it proved too heavy for them to shift – twelve men would be needed – so they left it by the roadside. Sometimes a stone thrown by a giant still bears the marks of his hand or his fingerprints, to prove the truth of the story. One such boulder weighing several tons was lifted from the castle rock at Peel Castle (Isle of Man) by a giant who was terrorizing the island, and thrown half a mile to the opposite hill, bearing ever afterwards his handprint; while a Hampshire giant known as Onion is said to have thrown the Imp Stone about a mile from Silchester to its resting place beside the road on the Hampshire/Berkshire boundary, leaving his fingerprints on it.

As there are so many accounts of stones bearing visible evidence of superbeings – footprints and kneeprints in addition to fingerprints and handprints, and horses' hoofprints – we will return to these later in this chapter. But first some more stones which were thrown, this time by the Devil. He threw a boulder across the River Tay, aiming for the giant of Law Hill, Dundee (Angus), but it fell short, landing elsewhere in Dundee and acquiring the logical name of the De'il's Stane. He also threw the rocks in the Valley of Stones on Blackdown (Dorset), as well as the Agglestone*, a 20-foot rock weighing 400 tons on Studland Heath. This was also known as the Devil's Nightcap, and he was sitting on the Needles off the Isle of Wight when he threw it. Very often the Devil was aiming at a religious building when he threw a rock, and in this case it may have been Salisbury Cathedral. If so, the rock thankfully fell well short. The same thing happened in Somerset when the Devil was intending to demolish Cranmore church: the rock he threw landed in Hurdlestone Woods near Stoke St Michael and lies on the edge of a cliff there. In Cheshire he was again a bad shot. The rock he threw at Acton church while it was being built landed in a field near Bluestone. The Hell Stone which gave its name to Helston (Cornwall) was broken up and built into the wall of the Angel Hotel, but originally it was brought from Hell by the Devil, and dropped here when he was challenged to a battle by his old

enemy St Michael the Archangel. In Gwent, the Devil tried to prevent St Cadoc from building a church on the Lasgarn Mountain, by pulling down at night what the saint had built during the day, and also by fetching an apron-load of rocks to drop on the building. St Cadoc decided to make a bell to ward off the enemy, and just as the Devil was about to drop his rocks on the church, the bell rang out, the sound causing him to dump the rocks and flee. They now form a rocky pile known as Garn Clochdy or the belltower cairn.

The throwing of rocks was not solely the pastime of giants and the Devil. Even saints did it sometimes. St Mawes was preaching one day by the sea when a noisy seal interrupted him, and in anger he threw a rock at the animal. Fortunately it missed, and landed on top of Black Rocks in Falmouth Harbour (Cornwall). A witch threw the Saville Stone at Scar, Sanday (Orkney), aiming for but missing her daughter and her lover. King Arthur threw a stone from his chair on King's Crags near Sewingshields (Northumberland) when he was quarrelling with his queen Guinevere as she sat on Queen's Crags opposite him. But it hit her comb and landed harmlessly between the two sandstone outcrops, the comb's toothmarks visible on it.

All the tales so far have described rocks deliberately thrown, but often they were dropped by accident. The Witch's Stone in Glenfernate (Inverness/Perth) was fetched by her from the Isle of Man after she had promised to build a castle in Badenoch. She was flying back with it at dawn, when a hunter saw the dark mass in the sky and cried out 'God bless us!' This caused her to lose her magic powers and the rock fell from her apron to the ground, where it lies to this day, all 1,000 tons of it. The Devil was trying to build a bridge linking England with the Isle of Man when he dropped the stone now known as Carl Crag. His bridge was to start at the Herdy Neb, a promontory near Seascale (Cumbria), but his apron-strings broke and he dropped the foundation stone a mile south of the Herdy Neb. It bears the marks of his apron-strings as two white stripes, but unfortunately the boulder is now covered by sand. His apron-strings also broke when he was

carrying stones over the Stiperstones* (Shropshire), scattering

them around his Chair. The White Rocks on Garway Hill (Herefordshire) were scattered when the Devil's apron-strings broke as he was carrying rocks to help Jack o' Kent block a weir so as to flood the valley for a fish pool. Before he could gather them up, the cock crew and he had to go home. In Durham his apron-strings broke yet again, dropping a stone he was carrying into Castle Eden Dene; and rocks from a giant's creel were spilt at the southern end of Greeba (Isle of Man).

As mentioned earlier, a number of stones bear marks which act as confirmation of the stories told about them. There are many footprints, mainly the Devil's but other people's too, such as Owain Glyndwr, the Welsh folk hero whose footprint is still to be seen in his home area of Corwen* (Clwyd) on a hill above the town; the Virgin Mary whose footprint is on a rock above Llanfair near Harlech (Gwynedd); and a giant whose footprint can be seen on a rock near Boscawen-Un stone circle (Cornwall). The Devil's footprints can be found at places as far apart as Llanymynech Hill in Shropshire, the Rock of the Evil One on Cadair Idris (Gwynedd) where he danced, the Crag of the Oxen overlooking Alwen Reservoir (Clwyd) where he dug in his heels as he was being dragged from Cerrigydrudion church by two oxen and finally submerged in Llyn-dau-Ychain on the Denbigh Moors, and the Devil's Stone above Birtley (Northumberland). From this stone high above a valley, he tried to leap across to Lee Hall on the other side of the Tyne, but he fell into the so-called Leap Crag Pool and was drowned.

Other parts of the Devil's and other people's anatomy have also left marks on stones; for example, in a rock pool called the Pot o' Pittentyoul in a stream passing the Dhu Craig near Newmill, Keith (Banff), hollows in the rocks are said to mark the place where the Devil sat. His right kneecap and left foot are on a hillside near Llanblethian (South Glamorgan), where St Quintin lamed him, while St Cynwal left his knee marks in rocks beside a river at Cynwyl Gaio (Dyfed) where he knelt to pray. Farmers would take their cattle to the hollows and pour the water from them over the animals in order to keep them healthy in the coming year. A stone near the Roman gold mines at Dolaucothi*

(Dyfed) was a pillow for five saints sleeping in the mine tunnels, and their heads have left depressions in the stone. King Arthur's knee- and finger-marks are said to be visible on a boulder lying near the prehistoric stone burial chamber called Arthur's Stone above Dorstone (Herefordshire), left there when he lifted the boulder and placed it in position on the stone uprights of the burial chamber; though there is no evidence that the boulder ever formed part of that monument. In another version, the hollows to be seen on the boulder are the marks of Arthur's knees after he knelt on it to pray; or are the marks of a giant's elbows, left when he fell on to the stone when killed by Arthur. St Agnes Well at Chapel Porth (Cornwall) was also known as Giant's Well, from the time when the giant Bolster, striding between Carn Brea and St Agnes Beacon, stopped to drink from the well and left the marks of his fingers on one of the stones. Robin Hood left his fingermarks on a stone which he threw and which landed in the River Tame near Arden Mill (Cheshire): like King Arthur and other folk heroes he sometimes took on the role of a giant. An Orkney giant left his fingerprints on a stone he threw from the island of Westray to the island of Rousay. Known afterwards as the Finger Steen, it stood on the cliff edge at the Leean and fishermen who passed it would place a pebble in the fingermarks to ensure a good catch of fish and to avert disaster.

Animals have also left their marks on rocks, usually horses' hoofprints, but one tale from Norfolk describes how a miraculous cow gave milk to all the poor people at a time of famine. When the famine was over, she struck her foot on a sandstone slab and vanished. The Oxfoot Stone is at South Lopham. Marks in a rocky stream bed at Upper Sapey near Bromyard (Herefordshire) are said to be the footprints of St Catharine Audley's mare and colt, the horse having carried St Catharine to Ledbury. In one version, the animals were stolen and St Catharine prayed that wherever the animals trod, their footmarks would be left, and so they, and the marks of the pattens worn by the girl thief, were followed and the animals recovered. In one version of this tale, the thief was turned to stone and became the Hoar Stone. The marks were in fact made by the

action of the water upon the stone of the stream bed. The hoof-mark of a horse belonging to a little-known Welsh saint, Engan or Einion Frenhin, was left on a stone near Castell Cilan, Llanengan (Gwynedd), and the water which gathers in the depression was believed to cure warts. A modern alternative explanation for the hoofprint was that a doctor was galloping home from visiting a patient and, somewhat the worse for drink, he was going the wrong way, towards the cliffs. His horse knew, and came to a sudden halt in the nick of time, leaving its hoofprint on the rock.

St George's horse left its hoofprints on a stone at St George (Clwyd) when the saint slew the dragon there, and King Arthur's horse left its hoofprints in several places, including a rock on Carn March Arthur, a hill above Aberdyfi (Gwynedd), when Arthur came to Llyn Barfog to kill a monster; and also on a stone on Goss Moor, Arthur's favourite hunting-ground near St Columb Major (Cornwall), where the king's horse left four prints. King Arthur fought a battle against a Saxon army on Moel Arthur, a hill in the Clwydian range, and when he was about to be killed, Arthur's horse made a mighty leap and carried him to safety, leaving its hoofmarks on a stone at the place, now to be found beside the road at Loggerheads* (Clwyd). Sometimes the hoofprints are said to be those of the Devil's horse, as at the Devil's Doorway, a fault in the slate rocks behind Polperro (Cornwall) which was said to be a way into the underworld, and where the Devil's horse left its hoofmark as he carried the Devil through. When in Devon, His Satanic Majesty and his Wild Hunt would haunt the Dewer Stone on the southern edge of Dartmoor, trying to lure people to the edge of the cliff so that they would fall into the river below. One morning, or so it was said, the imprint of a naked human foot was found at the edge of the Dewer Stone, with cloven hooves visible behind it.

The shapes of some stones suggested what their former uses might have been. There are many stones which have been given the name of someone's chair or seat, for example King Fingal's Seat at the north-western end of Loch Ashie (Inverness). This is a large boulder at a place where the king is said to have fought a

111

battle, and there is also a tradition of phantom armies being seen here after dawn on May Day. Madgy Figgy's Chair is a rock on Chair Ladder south-west of St Levan (Cornwall) where the witch of that name would sit and watch the storms raging at sea, and ships being wrecked, probably having previously cast spells to raise the winds. The Devil would sit on his chair on Largo Law, a rocky hill in Fife, or on another of his chairs atop the Stiperstones* in Shropshire. Among the many giants' chairs are one in a cliff at Kirksanton (Cumbria), Cadair Idris (Idris's Chair) on top of the mountain of that name (Gwynedd), and Cadair Fronwen, a stone pile acting as the chair of the giant Bronwen on top of the Berwyn Mountains (Clwyd/Powys).

The many saints who lived in the rural areas of Britain also had rock seats, for example Eisteddfa Grannog (Carannog's Seat), a large chair-shaped rock above the harbour at Llangrannog (Dyfed); Cadair Gawrdaf (Cawrdaf's Chair), a large boulder with a seat cut into it, located about a quarter-mile from Abererch church (Gwynedd); Cadair Gybi (Cybi's Chair)*, a rock on the wooded hillside above the saint's well at Llangybi (Gwynedd); and Cadair Dydecho, St Tydecho's chair at Llanymawddwy (Gwynedd). St Fillan's Seat on Dunfillan at Comrie (Perth) was used as a cure for backache, sufferers climbing up the hill to sit in the seat and then being pulled downhill by their ankles. Canna's Chair in a field by the old church of Llangan (Dyfed) was also used for healing purposes, the nearby holy well being visited by people suffering from ague and intestinal complaints. They would drink a specified quantity of the well water, and also sometimes bathe in the well, then sit in the chair for a while, a cure being more likely if the patient slept while in the chair. The ritual would be continued for days, sometimes for two or three weeks. A hollowed-out rock known as Clach-na-Bhan (Stone of the Woman) on top of Meall-ghaineah, a hill on the east side of Glen Avon (Banff), was visited by pregnant women, who sat in the seat to ensure an easy delivery. Single women also came, believing that contact with the stone would help them find a husband. When the details of usage of a stone

chair, or a holy well, are forgotten, it often becomes known

simply as a wishing chair, or a wishing well. The natural rock seat known as the Wishing Chair on Overton Hills (Cheshire) may once have had a more specific role assigned to it.

Some rocks look more like beds than chairs, hence such names as Gwely Melangell (St Melangell's Bed), a rock shelf in woods near Pennant Melangell church (Powys), and Gwely Tydecho (St Tydecho's Bed), a rock shelf in the hills above Llanymawddwy (Gwynedd). Arthur's Bed is a stone on Bodmin Moor (Cornwall) naturally hollowed out into a coffin shape. Such rocks in giant country are known as Giant's Coffin, as on Carn Brea Hill (Cornwall), or Giantess's Cradle (Crud y Gawres), as at Ardudwy (Gwynedd). Some hollows were seen as the cooking utensils of the superbeings, as for example the Devil's Frying Pan, which was a natural rock basin near Mis Tor on Dartmoor (Devon), and Arthur's Pot, a stone made by Merlin in which to cook the king's dinner, on the banks of the River Tawe near Dolwilym (West Glamorgan). In Northumberland, the fairies made holes for porridge pots in the rocks by Hart Burn near Rothley.

Sometimes a quite elaborate story has been woven round a site, as for example The Wrekin* in Shropshire, where several notable features were formed by giants, including a rock basin on the summit which is known as the Raven's Bowl, or the Cuckoo's Cup. When the giants were fighting, a raven flew up and pecked at the eyes of the one who was winning, and he shed a huge tear that fell on the rock and hollowed out the basin. It is said to be always full of water, even in the driest summer, and it was once customary to taste the water when climbing The Wrekin. It is probable that this was once done for a specific purpose, but what that was has not been recorded. Also on the Wrekin is the Needle's Eye, a cleft in the rock said to have been cut by a giant's spade, again when the giants were quarrelling. It was once the proper thing for a girl, on her first visit, to squeeze through the gap. Her boyfriend would (or should) be waiting on the other side, and would demand something coloured from her clothing as a forfeit. If she looked back while passing through the gap, she would never be married. The details that have survived suggest

113

that this was once a fertility ritual of some kind. People would also crawl through a Needle's Eye on the Stiperstones* (Shropshire).

The unusual shapes of stones have triggered off some very fanciful names and stories. At Tintagel* (Cornwall), where the King Arthur story overshadows the place's real history, numerous features associated with the legend can be seen at the king's so-called birthplace: his footprint, his seat, his window, his bed/elbow-chair/hip-bath, his cups and saucers, and a large rock 'portrait'. In other places, natural rock formations also have the appearance of large stone heads, as for example St Tydecho's Head on the hillside above Llanymawddwy (Gwynedd), Bowerman's Nose* on Dartmoor (Devon) and The Old Man of Mow, a rock pillar resembling a man's head near to the castle on Mow Cop (Staffordshire).

Some rock formations with a vague resemblance to human figures are said to be people turned to stone for various reasons. Four pillar-like stones at Dawnton Castle near Ludlow (Shropshire) were four women turned to stone because they danced with the Devil. The Naked Boy on the Brendon Hills (Somerset) was turned to stone for drunkenness, and as a penance must go at midnight to a nearby spring to drink. A limestone pillar above the Clydach Gorge (Gwent) is known as The Lonely Shepherd, turned to stone for his cruelty to his wife who ended her life in the River Usk. He must now go down to the river at midnight each Midsummer Night to search for his wife, returning to the mountain at dawn. Stones beside Brightstone/ Bridestone Lane at Farringdon (Hampshire) are a young man and his bride, turned to stone for an unspecified reason as they strolled along the lane on Good Friday. Also seen as a man and his wife were two rock pillars at Storr on the Isle of Skye, though the wife has now fallen (*see plate 21*). The surviving pillar is known as The Old Man of Storr. They were searching for a lost cow when they met giants who turned them to stone. Am Bodach (The Old Man) and A'Chailleach (The Old Woman) are two rock pillars above Loch Eanaich in the Cairngorms (Inverness). There was enmity between them, and when a thunderstorm

raged in the mountains, the two were said to be having a fight. The cliff headlands known as the Suitors of Cromarty (Ross and Cromarty) were two giant brothers turned to stone for transgressing some ancient law. The hoofprints of magician Michael Scot's horse can be seen on both the Suitors, left there after he leapt from one to the other when fleeing from his demons who constantly begged him to give them more work to do.

Wherever there is a collection of unusually shaped rocks, it seems impossible to resist giving them outlandish names, vaguely based on their appearance. In Devon, the Valley of Rocks on the north coast near Lynton has The Thinker (alternatively The Drummer or The Drinker), the Devil's Cheesewring (or Cheese Knife), The Castle, and Ragged Dick, the last being a man and his friends turned to stone by the Devil for dancing on a Sunday. In North Yorkshire, Brimham Rocks* overlooking Nidderdale are strange rock formations given names like Druid's Altar, Druid's Skull and Druid's Head, from the supposed pagan rituals that were said to have been performed there, and others are named from their appearances the Dancing Bear, Baboon, Chimney Rock, Pivot Rock, and Yoke of Oxen. A group of rocks on Corn Ridge, Sourton Common, Dartmoor (Devon) are known as Branscombe's Loaf and Cheese, the story being that a thirteenth-century Bishop of Exeter who was riding home one summer evening with a servant was offered refreshment by a stranger they met on the moor. The Bishop accepted the round loaf and lump of cheese the man held out, but just before he took a bite his servant dashed the food from his hand. He had seen the stranger's cloven hooves peeping out from underneath his long cloak, and knew that if the Bishop ate the food, he would be in the Devil's power. The loaf and cheese were turned into huge rounded granite boulders, and not far away are the Slipper Stones, said in one story to have been the Bishop's slippers, and in another to have been the Devil's. He was taking a drink from the river just before he met the Bishop, and one shoe was washed away when he caught his foot in the river stones.

A stone above Staunton (Gloucestershire) is sometimes called the Frog or Toad's Mouth because it resembles the head and

gaping jaw of a monster. A stone in a wall in Braddan (Isle of Man) looks like a saddle, and indeed there is a story explaining how it became known as the Fairy Saddle. A Vicar of Braddan found that his horse was being taken out of the field at night, and in the morning would be tired and sweating heavily, as if having been ridden all night. Early one morning the vicar saw a little man in a green jacket carrying a riding whip, turning the horse loose into the field. When he saw the vicar, he vanished, leaving the saddle which he had placed by the fence. This turned to stone, and has been there ever since. The Sack Stone, or Stone Sack, at Fonaby near Caistor (Lincolnshire) was believed to be a petrified sack of corn, turned to stone by Christ who came by one day and saw men sowing corn. They did not know who he was, and when he asked for grain for his ass, they said they had none. Asking what was in the sack, and being told 'Stones', he said 'Stone be it!' It was believed to be bad luck to interfere with the stone, the farmers who worked the land where it stood reporting illness and death if it were moved.

The Sack Stone, until it was split up and put under the hedge early this century, had to be left severely alone or else problems would arise. Some stones, on the other hand, were believed to be able to move of their own accord. The top stone of The Cheesewring* on Bodmin Moor (Cornwall) was said to turn three times when the cock crowed (*see plate 23*). A number of standing stones were also said to turn at the same time, and in some cases this happened when they *heard* the cock crow, as with the stone known as the Whirl Stone, several tons in weight and located in a brook at The Beach near Marton (Shropshire). Of course stones can't hear anything, and the use of this detail was probably meant to suggest that the rest of the story, about the stones moving, was equally nonsensical! The Wych Boulder near Orby (Lincolnshire) was a large pear-shaped stone which was said to turn over when the clock struck twelve, while the Whetstone on the summit of Hergest Ridge near Kington (Herefordshire) was said to go down to the water to drink every morning when it heard the cock crow. The Bambury or Banbury Stones on Bredon Hill (Worcestershire) would go down to the

Avon to drink when they (or it – there was one stone until the nineteenth century, when movement of the ground split it) heard the church clock strike midnight, or when it heard the bells of Pershore Abbey.

In a variation of the drinking stories, it was believed in connection with a stone called The Devil's Pulpit at Tealby (Lincolnshire) that it was the *Devil* who went to drink at the stream when he heard the clock strike twelve, and children would keep away for fear they might meet him. The stone's name suggests that there was also once a legend that the Devil used the stone as a pulpit, as he did with another Devil's Pulpit* near Tintern (which town is in Gwent, but the pulpit is in Gloucestershire). It was a crag near the Abbey, and he would use it to spy on the Abbot and preach at the monks. When he went down among them, they showered him with holy water and he fled, leaving the marks of his talons on a stone at Llandogo. There was also a Devil's Pulpit at Hemswell (Lincolnshire), a natural rock slab above a group of springs. Other stones used as pulpits include Maen Sigl or St Tudno's Cradle, on the Great Orme at Llandudno (Gwynedd), from which the saint is said to have preached; and Huw Lloyd's Pulpit*, a rock in the River Cynfal below Ffestiniog (Gwynedd) used by a wizard and prophet to call up the dead.

As was briefly touched on earlier in this chapter, rituals were performed at some stones, sometimes simply because that was the thing to do, the original significance of the act having been long forgotten, but sometimes with a definite purpose in view, such as a cure for some illness or to keep evil spirits at bay. The Twelve O'Clock Stone near Nancledra (Cornwall) was believed to be able to cure children of rickets, and as its name suggests the timing was important. The stone could rock like a cradle, but only at midnight, and it was then that children were placed naked on the stone. The stone would not move nor the ritual work if the child had dissolute parents. The Tolmen was a holed stone in the bed of the Teign River on Dartmoor (Devon), and a cure for rheumatism was said to be achieved by climbing through the hole on to the stone slab beneath. Faithless wives

also had to climb through the stone, as part of a purification ritual. People were passed between the King and Queen Stones on Bredon Hill (Worcestershire) to restore them to health, or through the forked rock called the Crick Stone at Morvah (Cornwall) which cured 'crick in the back' if you didn't touch the stone while passing through, while sick children were passed over the huge Drake Stone* above Harbottle (Northumberland). The Kelpie Stone or Needle in the River Dee near Dinnet (Aberdeen) had the power to confer fertility, if the childless woman passed through an 18-inch diameter hole in the stone, and in the same direction as the flow of the river.

There were many other healing stones, but often they were manually erected in prehistoric times, and so are not the naturally occurring features which are the subject of this book. Without having seen the stones, it is often impossible to know whether a prehistoric standing stone or a natural stone is being described in a folklorist's account. The problem is illustrated in accounts of the ritual of pouring milk on to a certain stone as an offering for a spirit: are these named stones prehistoric standing stones or not? On the island of Iona (Argyll) the women used to pour milk on to the Glaistig's Stone at milking time each evening, in order to propitiate the glaistig (usually half-woman, half-goat) who lived in a hollow rock nearby. There was another Glaistig's Stone in Glen Duror of Appin (Argyll), where libations of milk were also poured each evening, and this glaistig's self-appointed role was to keep the calves from suckling their mothers during the night, so that there was milk for the breakfast porridge. When a new tenant failed to provide the libations, the glaistig let the calves mix with the cows and there was no milk at breakfast. On Vallay off North Uist, milk had to be poured on to a certain flat stone every Sunday to keep happy a gruagach (means 'hairy one', and can either be female and like a glaistig, or male, often performing farm work), who was angered when an attempt was made to plough the island.

Witches featured in the rituals once practised at some stones. There was a Witches' Rock near Zennor (Cornwall) where all the witches of the neighbourhood used to meet on Midsummer Eve.

If you touched the rock nine times at midnight, you would be protected against evil and bad luck. There is a Witch's Stone in Westleton churchyard (Suffolk), and children used to run round the church three (or seven) times after placing something in the grating in the wall above the stone. At the end of the run, the object should have disappeared; or rattling chains might be heard. A similar stone in the churchyard at Bungay (Suffolk) was known as the Druid Stone* (or Devil's Stone, or Giant's Grave), and it was customary to run round it twelve times (or dance around it seven times) after calling on the Devil to appear. An alternative ritual was to knock on the stone seven times on a certain day and wait for the Devil to appear, or knock on it and place your ear to the stone to hear the answers to your questions. Similarly, children would prick pins into the little hollows on the surface of the Bound Stone at Hemswell (Lincolnshire) and then run fast round the stone. Finally they would put their ears to it and listen to hear the Devil speak!

The Devil's Stone at Shebbear (Devon) has several connections with His Satanic Majesty. In one story he is buried underneath it; in another he dropped it when fleeing from Heaven, after he had been thrown out. A strange old custom is performed at the stone annually on 5 November, when bell-ringers using crowbars turn over the 1-ton stone. This is done to keep the Devil away for another year. When the stone was not turned one year during the First World War, bad luck followed for the village. The church bells are rung before the stone is turned, and this is traditionally a means of keeping evil spirits at bay. In Lincolnshire the Winceby Boulder at Winceby was said to guard hidden treasure, and no one could move it. One farmer put chains round it and pulled with his horses. As it began to move, one of the helpers said, 'Let God or the Devil come now for we have it!' At which the stone fell back into its former immovable position, the Devil having put in a brief appearance, and left a claw-mark on the stone to prove it. The stone was later buried in a hole dug beside it.

The Devil used to provide the music for the witches' sabbat every 12 May (old May Day) at The Harp, a rock on the shore of

Loch Ness (Inverness) near Tychat farm. He was also said to be responsible for the mysterious removal of the Stone of Petti, an 8-ton boulder which used to stand 400-500 yards inland on the coast of the Bay of Petti (Moray), until the stormy night of 20 February 1799. Next morning it was found to have moved 260 yards out to sea, an event said to have been foretold by the prophet known as the Brahan Seer. A stone which was said to have come back to land out of the sea was Maen Morddwyd, or the Thigh Stone, so-called because it resembled a human thigh. It was kept in the old parish church of Llanidan, Brynsiencyn, on the island of Anglesey (Gwynedd), and in the reign of Henry the First, Hugh, Earl of Chester, decided to test its supposed ability to miraculously return from wherever it was taken. He had it chained to a larger stone and thrown into the sea, but next morning it was found to be back in its usual place. Other stones which were said to be able to return were Smig Mhic Mharcuis (The Chin of Mac Marquis), a piece of basalt which until early this century lay on a flat stone tomb in Kilbrandon graveyard on Seil in the Slate Isles (Argyll); and also a stone bearing the footprint of King Arthur's dog Cabal, which lay on a heap of stones known as Carn Cabal on the mountain near Rhayader (Powys). Reminiscent of the Stone of Petti, there is a stone north of Stockton village (Warwickshire) that was said to have been carried from Mountsorrel (Leicestershire) by the waters of the Flood.

It was not only the Devil who was the key figure in the folklore of rocks and stones. A prominent cleft stone in the churchyard at St Levan* (Cornwall) was said to have been split in two by the saint himself. It was his favourite seat after returning from fishing, so before he died he split it open with his fist and prophesied (or alternatively it was Merlin who said):

> *When with panniers astride,*
> *A packhorse one can ride*
> *Through St Levan's Stone,*
> *The world will be done.*

The Cloven Stones at Baldrine (Isle of Man) were split by one blow of King Orry's sword, or alternatively by the power of Christianity overcoming paganism, and they were said to clap together when the church bells ring. It was a giant who split a stone on the Denbigh Moors (Clwyd). It stands about 7 feet high, east of the site called Hen Ddinbych, and a large fragment of the stone lies beside it, supposedly sliced off by a giant with a sword, hence the stone's name of Maen y Cleddau (The Stone of the Sword).

The Bonnet Stone in Kinveachy Woods (Inverness) concealed a giant's heart, placed there by him in order to stop people killing him. The only way to kill him was for a man to lay his bonnet on the stone while the heart was in it, whereupon it would die. If the giant saw a man wearing a bonnet anywhere near the stone, he would quickly take his heart and hide it in a different stone. An evil spirit or mischievous goblin which haunted the Llanwddyn valley (Powys), where the reservoir known as Lake Vyrnwy now stands, was caught and placed under a large stone in the river, which was then called Carreg yr Yspryd or Ghost Stone. He was told to stay under the stone until water should lie between the stone and dry land, but no one then realized that before too long, the valley would be flooded to make the reservoir. When the time came to destroy the 15-20-ton stone, the local people were somewhat nervous that the evil spirit would be released. The workmen dynamited the stone, and all present saw a large frog sitting calmly in front of the debris, rubbing its eyes as if waking from a long sleep, and they wondered if it was the spirit in disguise. If it was merely a frog, why had it not been destroyed in the explosion? No one dared approach it, but eventually it was driven away and work continued, but for nights afterwards, or so it was said, the sound of heavy chains dragging along the ground could be heard where the stone had stood.

We have now come to the end of our survey of the folklore and legends linked with Britain's natural landscape features, but we do so with the realization that we have merely scratched the surface, and each reader will no doubt be aware of many other

places that we could have included. Nevertheless we hope we have given a true taste of this rich and varied folklore, and we also hope that some of our readers will have been fired with enthusiasm and will want to go exploring. Anyone who does want to take a closer look at the places we have mentioned will find some of the most interesting described in more detail in *Places to Visit* which follows.

Places to Visit

The sites are arranged by county,
in alphabetical order.

CHESHIRE

....

Alderley Edge

This wooded sandstone escarpment is now an attractive place to walk (*see plate 22*), but in past centuries it has been well used for industrial purposes, as the surviving quarry sites and mining tunnels testify. Earlier still, prehistoric man lived here. Traces of a large Neolithic settlement have been found, and Bronze Age tools and pottery. In folklore, it is one of the many places in Britain where King Arthur and his men were said to lie sleeping, only waking when their country needs them. One day, a farmer actually saw them. He was taking a white horse over the Edge to sell it in the market, and refused an offer from an old man, who said he would not sell it that day. Sure enough, in the

evening the farmer led the unsold horse back over the Edge, and again met the old man. He followed him to a rock, which the old man touched, and a set of iron gates opened up. The old man, who was in fact Merlin, King Arthur's wizard, showed the farmer that inside the hillside were caverns filled with sleeping men and white horses. He said that they were King Arthur and his knights, and that they needed another horse to make up the numbers. He offered a purse of gold, which the farmer snatched as he ran from the cave. The gates closed behind him, and have never been seen again.

Merlin's presence on the Edge is remembered in The Wizard Restaurant on the Macclesfield Road; and also in the Wizard's Well, a wishing well on the Edge where water drips off the rock into a trough. An inscription on the rock reads: 'Drink of this and take thy fill, for the water falls by the wizard's will'. There is also a carved face, but no one knows how old it is or who it is meant to represent. Merlin himself?

Alderley Edge is 4 miles north-west of Macclesfield. It is in the care of the National Trust, but always open, and there are car parks.

CLWYD

··

Carreg Carn March Arthur, Loggerheads

In the centre of this stone is a depression said to be the hoof-print of King Arthur's horse, Llamrei. It dates from the time when Arthur fought a battle against a Saxon army on the hill Moel Arthur in the Clwydian Range. He was being chased by the Saxons, straight towards the edge of a precipice and his life was in danger. His magical horse leapt out into space, and came to rest on this stone, leaving the mark of his hoof.

The Stone of Arthur's Horse's Hoof is underneath the Denbigh/Flint boundary marker, beside the Mold to Ruthin road at Loggerheads, up the hill from the entrance to the Country Park.

•••••••••••••••••••••••••••••••••••••

Dinas Bran, Llangollen

This prominent hill in the Vale of Llangollen is capped by the ruins of a medieval castle. A golden harp is said to be hidden in the hill, which can only be found by a boy who has a white dog with a silver eye. Dinas Bran has Arthurian connections, in that Bran was a legendary hero whose buried head King Arthur dug out of its resting place at Tower Hill in London, where it was said to protect the kingdom against invasion, so long as it remained buried. The Holy Grail – the vessel which Christ used at the Last Supper and which was supposedly brought to Britain by Joseph of Arimathea who went to Glastonbury and built the first church there – is perhaps hidden in the hill of Dinas Bran (*see also Glastonbury Tor, Somerset*), and it is interesting that Llangollen has an unusual link with Glastonbury. The name 'Llangollen' indicates that St Collen was active here, and he was the same saint who lived on Glastonbury Tor and met the king of the fairies there.

Fairies are also said to have been seen around Dinas Bran. A young lad called Tudur who was watching sheep on the hillside was drawn into the fairy dance one summer's night. The scene was a hollow called Nant yr Ellyllon (goblins' brook), halfway up the hillside. First Tudur saw a tiny man with a fiddle, then the dancers arrived and the music began. Tudur was entranced by the scene, though he hesitated about joining in for fear that the Devil might be responsible and he would be spirited away. However, he couldn't resist, and as he danced he cried, 'Play away, old devil; brimstone and water, if you like!' As soon as he spoke, the musician turned into the Devil and the fairies became animals, and as they danced they looked like a wheel of fire.

Tudur danced all night because he could not stop and his master, searching for the lost sheep and their shepherd, came upon him still spinning around in the hollow.

A footpath from the north of the town of Llangollen leads up to the top of Dinas Bran. The stiff climb is well worth it for the extensive views from the top in clear weather.

····································

Owain Glyndwr's Footprint, Corwen

Owain Glyndwr (Owen Glendower) was a fourteenth-fifteenth century popular hero who had claims to be regarded as a rightful Prince of Wales. He fought against the English in north-east Wales, and the area around Corwen still retains numerous links with his story. Owain Glyndwr's Mount is said to be the site of his manor-house, and Glyndwr's Seat is a viewpoint overlooking the town, on the hill Pen-y-Pigyn. A cross carved over the church's south door is known as Owain Glyndwr's Dagger, and was said to have been thrown by him from the hill. His footprint can be seen on rocks close to his seat.

Corwen is on the A5, 10 miles west of Llangollen. There is a good, if steep, footpath to Pen-y-Pigyn from the town centre, up the lane behind the Post Office and into the woods.

····································

St Winefride's Well, Holywell

Of the many surviving holy wells in Great Britain, this must surely be the most impressive (*see plate 10*). A very elaborate building with a chapel above was built over the well between 1495 and 1510, and a large outdoor bathing pool was constructed in the seventeenth century. All the buildings are well preserved, and indeed the well is still used for healing purposes. Numerous

pilgrimages assemble at the well each year, and there is still great interest in the cult of St Winefride, this having been given a boost recently with the discovery of a piece of the original wooden tent-shaped reliquary which housed the saint's relics, known as the Arch Gwenfrewi (St Winefride's Coffer). It has been dated to the mid-eighth century.

The story of the well's formation is that Winefride or Winifred (whose real, Welsh, name was Gwenfrewi) was the niece of St Beuno who was one day preaching at the chapel. Gwenfrewi was at home alone when Caradog, a local prince, arrived to see her father. Being captivated by Gwenfrewi, he expressed a desire to possess her, but she refused his demands (the original Latin suggests that a violent rape took place). She ran towards the chapel, whereupon he struck off her head with his sword. Her body fell outside the chapel and her head inside; or in another version, the fatal blow took place on the hillside above the chapel, and her head rolled down to the chapel door. When he saw what had happened, Beuno asked God not to spare Caradog, who promptly melted away. Beuno replaced Gwenfrewi's head and covered her with his mantle while he went back into the chapel to finish the mass, but when he had finished, she got up, completely restored to life. Since then there was always a thin line around her neck, and this is shown in depictions of her, in statues or stained-glass windows. Where her head came to rest, a spring began to flow, this holy well now being known as St Winefride's Well.

The water still runs very strongly, bubbling up into a star-shaped pool under the chapel. It flows into the outdoor bathing pool, where can be seen a stone in the water by the steps known as Maen Beuno (St Beuno's Stone). He is supposed to have sat here when instructing Gwenfrewi, and today pilgrims kneel on the stone after going through the inner well three times. This ritual may have originated in the Celtic baptismal rite of triple immersion. St Beuno's Stone was said to be stained with Gwenfrewi's blood, as were other smaller stones in the well, though this colouring was in fact caused by a type of lichen. A fragrant moss which grew in the well was known as

St Winefride's Hair. The well has been in regular use since the seventh century, and very many cures have been recorded. There still survives a pile of old crutches and surgical boots, discarded and left as offerings by people who were cured after visiting St Winefride's Well. So many cures were reported during the last century that the town of Holywell became known as 'The Lourdes of Wales'.

Holywell is in north-east Clwyd, 15 miles north-west of Chester, and the well is signposted. There is room to park in a lay-by opposite; a small entrance fee is payable.

CORNWALL

....

The Cheesewring

This strange rock formation perched above an old quarry out on Bodmin Moor was given its fanciful name from its imagined resemblance to the results of the Devil's attempts at cheese-making (*see plate 23*). The topmost stone was said to turn three times when it heard the cock crow. It was also said that you could sit in a natural stone chair beside it and talk to the Devil.

The Cheesewring is a walk of about a mile north from Minions, a small village 9 miles south-west of Launceston. (SX 258725)

....

Dozmary Pool

Prehistoric man of the Mesolithic period has left traces of his dwellings on the shore of Dozmary Pool out on Bodmin Moor. In the centuries since, this atmospheric place, especially when shrouded in winter mists, has become the focus of a variety

of folk beliefs. It was once thought to be bottomless, but since it dried up in 1859 that belief is no longer repeated! Perhaps the task given by a parson to the ghost of Jan Tregeagle, a villainous local magistrate in the seventeenth century, to empty the pool using a limpet shell with a hole in it, did not prove to be so impossible after all. Dozmary Pool is most famous as one of the places where King Arthur's sword Excalibur was thrown when he was mortally wounded in the Battle of Camlann. The King ordered his knight Sir Bedivere to throw the sword into the water, which he finally did, and a hand came out to catch it. It is not obvious why Dozmary Pool is a candidate for this legend, because it is not close to the supposed battle site. Yet there is a hint of ritual in the story, because the knight went three times to the water's side carrying the sword, but was loth to throw it away. But Arthur knew, because when he asked Bedivere what he saw, he reported only the lapping of the water. The King sent him again, and the third time Sir Bedivere did as Arthur had asked him, and threw away the sword. This time on returning to Arthur, he correctly told him that a hand had come out of the water and taken the sword, shaking it three times before taking it into the water. The repetition of threes is suggestive of some now-forgotten ritual.

Dozmary Pool is about 8 miles north-west of Liskeard, and close to a lane between St Neot and Bolventor (Jamaica Inn) (SX 195745).

···

Penhale Sands

This large area of sand dunes is said to conceal a town, buried in a storm as a punishment for the people's evil ways. Legend this may be, but in 1835 the remains of a very early church were uncovered, believed to be the church built by St Piran after he landed here from Ireland. Legend takes over again at this point, for the saint's voyage is said to have taken place on a millstone, to which he was chained before being thrown off the

cliffs into the sea off Ireland. Piran or Perran gave his name to Perranzabuloe (Piran-in-the-Sand) and Perranporth, and his cult flourished, both here and in Wales and Brittany. He was the patron saint of Cornish tin miners, and what were said to be his relics were kept in a nearby church and carried in processions. The remains of his church can be seen in the sand dunes, but the place now has no atmosphere because the ruins are covered by an ugly concrete structure. The site of his hermitage not far away is marked by an old Celtic stone cross, rather more in keeping with the Christian history embodied in this place.

Penhale Sands are immediately north of Perranporth, to the south-west of Newquay on the north-west coast. The oratory is roughly in the centre, and a path runs from a lane to the south-east. (Oratory O.S. map reference: SW 768564)

....

St Levan's Stone

This large cleft stone in the churchyard of St Levan was said to have been split by the saint himself. The stone was his favourite place to sit after he had been fishing, and he decided to make it his memorial stone. Having split it, he made a prophecy:

When with panniers astride,
A pack-horse one can ride
Through St Levan's stone,
The world will be done.

Fortunately there is still a long way to go before this prophecy is fulfilled. It seems likely that the stone had some importance at the time the church was built, for if it had not, it would surely have been destroyed or used in the building.

St Levan is in the furthest tip of Cornwall, only 3 miles south-east of Land's End, and the stone is close to the church door.

St Michael's Mount

Despite having been built on by man, St Michael's Mount is such an important legendary site that it is difficult to omit it from this book. According to legend, it was built by giant Cormoran who forced his wife to bring in the special stone he preferred. When he found she was bringing an inferior stone which she had found closer to hand, he kicked her and her apron-string broke, so that the stone fell to the ground and became Chapel Rock which can still be seen today. In another tale, she was killed by a blow from a hammer thrown by a giant who shared the use of one hammer with Cormoran, and they buried her beneath Chapel Rock.

The Mount is said to have once been surrounded by dry land with forests, though it is now an offshore island at high tide (*see plate 14*). The remains of fossilized trees have been found in Mount's Bay, to support the belief of an inundation by the sea at some point in the past. The Mount has long been regarded as a sacred place. A group of local fishermen are said to have had a vision in the year 495 on a rocky ledge near the top, during which the Archangel Michael appeared to them, and beginning its function as an important St Michael shrine. It has close links with Mont St Michel, a similar sacred rock off the north coast of France. The Benedictine monastery founded in 1044 was owned by the monks of Mont St Michel.

Miraculous healings are said to have occurred in the church built on the rock, a church which was demolished during an earthquake in 1275, the same earthquake that demolished the St Michael church on top of Glastonbury Tor in Somerset. While rebuilding was taking place, the skeleton of a huge man about 8 feet tall was discovered, and his 9 foot square tomb cut in the rock still exists near the chapel altar. In 1425 the Mount was taken over by the Crown and the monks turned out. A castle was built during the fourteenth century, and the Mount is now in the care of the National Trust. It is an important point on the St

Michael Line, the most famous 'ley line' in Britain, which stretches from south-west Cornwall to the Suffolk coast, passing through many St Michael sites on the way.

St Michael's Mount is in south-west Cornwall, in Mount's Bay just offshore from Marazion and a little east of Penzance. At low tide, access is on foot across a causeway; at high tide there is a ferry. Opening times vary, and there is an admission charge.

....

St Nectan's Glen

Deep in woodland a mysterious waterfall can be found, the water falling into a rock basin 20 feet deep and known as St Nectan's Kieve (basin). Nectan was a Celtic saint, said to have been a hermit who lived here in the fifth century in a sanctuary above the waterfall. According to tradition, a silver bell hung in his chapel and it would ring out in stormy weather when ships were wrecked on the nearby coast, calling for help from Tintagel Castle, for both castle and coast were visible from the chapel. As Nectan approached death, it was a turbulent time for the Christian religion, and he vowed that his silver bell would never ring for unbelievers, whereupon he dropped it into the kieve. Whenever the muffled sound of a ringing bell is heard, it is said to be St Nectan's silver bell, and a bad omen.

Two women, possibly the saint's sisters, are said to have buried him and his treasures in an oak chest underneath the kieve. Centuries later, some miners tried to recover the treasure by blasting into the rocks, but they stopped on hearing a silver bell, and a voice saying, 'The child is not yet born who shall recover this treasure.' Regardless of treasure, the glen and waterfall are well worth visiting for their wonderful atmosphere. The lane to the waterfall is said to be haunted, and in recent years someone living in the building on the site of the saint's hermitage met two figures approaching her at dusk as she strolled along the lane. She said good evening to them, and was surprised when they

failed to answer; even more surprised when they walked right through her and disappeared!

At Trethevy, a mile north-east of Tintagel on the Boscastle road, follow the lane that passes the holy well and little church, and continue on foot along the path through the woods and into the glen. An admission charge is payable to visit the waterfall. (SX 080885)

....

Tintagel Castle and Merlin's Cave

Tintagel Castle is traditionally King Arthur's birthplace, and many visitors come here specifically because of the Arthurian connection, though whether Tintagel has any link with him in reality is doubtful. Nevertheless numerous connections have been made in folklore, and both for these, and for the drama of the site, Tintagel is well worth visiting – preferably outside the tourist season, or early in the morning, because it can get very busy, and crowds of people spoil the atmosphere.

The places linked to the Arthurian legend are:

Merlin's Cave on the shore below the castle, and the place where Merlin is supposed to have taken the baby boy Arthur from the sea.

King Arthur's Footprint, a hollow in the rock at the highest point of the Island's southern side. This is not entirely natural, having been shaped by human hand at some stage, and it may have been used as a place of inauguration, where a king or chieftain had to stand during the ceremony.

King Arthur's Bed, Elbow Chair or Hip-Bath, a long hollow in the rock, again cut by human hand and probably originally intended as a grave in medieval times. It is located by the chapel, not far from the footprint.

King Arthur's Seat, Window, and Cups and Saucers, again not far from the footprint. The window is a slit in the rock, and the cups and saucers are hollows cut in the rock, either natural hollows 'improved' by man, or completely man-made.

Tintagel is on the north Cornish coast, about 14 miles north of Bodmin, and the Castle is easy to find from the village, being only a short walk away. In the care of English Heritage, and closed at certain times; admission fee payable.

··

Trencrom Hill

Trencrom (or Trecrobben) Hill was the site of a giant's castle, in the centre of an area overrun with giants, if names like Giant's Table, Giant's Round, Giant's Quoit, and so on, are anything to go by. They liked to play games with rocks which they threw around, and from Trencrom they would throw rocks at St Michael's Mount (a rocky outcrop situated just offshore). The Bowl Rock, at the foot of the hill, is one of their bowling balls.

The hill was also occupied by spriggans, who were a kind of fairy or, according to some people, the ghosts of giants, and their job was to guard the treasure hidden in the hill. One man who came out one night to dig for the treasure saw them coming out in swarms. They were small, but as they grew closer he could see that they were also growing larger, and they looked 'as ugly as if they would eat him'. He managed to escape, but was so shocked by his experience that he took to his bed.

Trencrom Hill is 3 miles south of St Ives. In National Trust care, several footpaths cross the hill. The Bowl Rock is 1/2 mile to the north-east.

DEVON

....

Bowerman's Nose

There probably never was a Mr Bowerman whom this natural rock formation resembled; the name may come from the Celtic *vawr-maen*, great stone. There was an unlikely story that Bowerman was St Winefride's father, turned to stone for hunting on a Sunday. His hounds were also petrified, as the nearby Hound Tor. Bowerman's Nose is a good example of man's instinctive search for patterns: pictures in the fire, castles in the clouds, stone heads (and noses) in the rocks – and people even claim to see a giant head, pyramids, and other 'man-made' artefacts on photographs of the surface of Mars!

Bowerman's Nose is on Hayne Down, Dartmoor, a mile south-west of Manaton, which is 9 miles north-west of Newton Abbot.

....

Lydford Gorge

The 1¹/₂ mile gorge provides a dramatic riverside walk to the 90 feet high White Lady waterfall, and through a steep-sided ravine of oak woods above the River Lyd, where the most spectacular pothole in the river is named the Devil's Cauldron. The name of the White Lady echoes the ghostly women in white sometimes seen beside water. There is a ghost here, of an old lady called Kitty, who has a red kerchief round her head. A pool at the foot of the waterfall is known as Kit's Steps, because it is here that the ghost is seen. There is also a story that another Kitty, a young lady, tried to leap on horseback across the gorge at this place. The horse landed safely, but Kitty was caught in tree branches and her body stayed there for some while before she was found. In 1968 a soldier returning to camp took a shortcut

135

through the gorge and disappeared. It was only weeks later that his body was found floating in the Devil's Cauldron.

Lydford Gorge is in the care of the National Trust, and is open daily. The walk is difficult in places. The main entrance is at the west end of Lydford village, halfway between Okehampton and Tavistock.

DORSET

....

The Agglestone

This 400-ton rock was said to be a missile thrown by the Devil at Corfe Castle, to which he had taken a dislike. He was sitting on the Needles off the Isle of Wight at the time. His aim was poor and the rock fell short, landing on Studland Heath. Other suggested targets include Bindon Abbey and Salisbury Cathedral. The stone has also been called the Devil's Anvil, from its shape, and the Devil's Nightcap.

The Agglestone, 17–20 feet tall, sits on the moor about a mile north-west of Studland, which is 2 miles north of Swanage. (SZ 023828)

DYFED

....

Carreg Pumpsaint, Dolaucothi

The Stone of the Five Saints is at Dolaucothi, the site of an ancient Roman gold mine, close to the village of Pumpsaint. The village name also means 'five saints', and this refers to quin-

tuplets named Gwyn, Gwynno, Gwynoro, Ceitho and Cynfelyn, who all became saints of the Celtic Church. According to legend, they are asleep in one of the tunnels of the gold mine: they took refuge there during a storm, laid down with their heads on a stone pillow, and fell asleep. They will not awake until King Arthur reappears, or a genuine and faithful apostolic bishop occupies the throne of St David. It was said that they wore hollows in the pillow, and turned it three times, finally throwing it out and taking a new one. The first pillow now stands upright near the entrance to the mines.

Pumpsaint is 7 miles south-east of Lampeter, and the gold mines, a National Trust property, are a mile to the east, at Dolaucothi. The stone can be seen on a grassy area near the car park and beside a lane. (SN 665405)

....

St Justinian's Well and Chapel

St Justinian was a sixth-century hermit and martyr of Ramsey Island off the Pembrokeshire coast, about whom various tales were told. It was said that he was killed by devils working through his three servants. When Justinian told them to work harder, they grew angry and cut off his head. They were struck down with leprosy as a punishment, while a healing spring began to flow where Justinian's head fell. Justinian carried his head across the sea to the place where he wished to be buried, and the remains of this chapel can still be seen, as can the holy well which sprang up where he put his head down. Chapel and well are at St Justinian, the site of a lifeboat station on the coast of Ramsey Sound, opposite Ramsey Island. The present chapel probably dates from the sixteenth century, but excavations have revealed much older remains, suggesting there has been a chapel here for over one thousand years.

St Justinian is 2 miles west of St David's. The well is beside the

road on the south side; the chapel is to the north, but on private land and can only be viewed from the road.

GLOUCESTERSHIRE

Devil's Pulpit, near Tintern

This rock outcrop looking like a pulpit is situated above the River Wye, with fine views over the valley. The Devil is said to have used it to preach to the monks at Tintern Abbey below. When he requested permission to go down and preach from their rood-loft, they surprisingly agreed, but as soon as he entered they showered him with holy water, causing him to take to his heels. He jumped over the river at Llandogo, leaving his claw marks on a rock there, as he fled into England.

4 miles north of Chepstow and a mile south-east of Tintern, the Devil's Pulpit is on the Offa's Dyke Path. Footpaths also lead to it from various directions, including Tintern. (ST 543996)

GWYNEDD

Bala Lake (Llyn Tegid)

This is the largest sheet of natural fresh water in Wales, covering 1084 acres and 140 feet deep in the centre. It covers an area roughly 4 miles long by 1 mile wide. Its Welsh name is said to come from Tegid Foel, the fifth-century lord of this region called Penllyn. He was the husband of Ceridwen who was in tradition the mother of Taliesin the seer. The lake is home to a rare fish, the gwyniad, which is a member of the salmon

family and found nowhere else. According to legend, the lake was formed when the cover was left off Ffynnon Gywer (Gower's Well) at Llangower on the south-east side of the lake. The old town of Bala was drowned, and it was said that the chimneys could be seen on clear days. A new town was built at the north of the lake, the present Bala, but legend prophesies that this town too will one day be submerged, and also the village of Llanfor further north.

Another story told how the old town was drowned because of the sinfulness of its inhabitants. A cruel prince who lived in one of the now-submerged palaces often heard a voice saying, 'Vengeance will come', but he ignored it. One day he was celebrating the birth of his grandson at a splendid feast, to which a harper had been brought. After playing for the dancing for some time, the harper had a rest about midnight, and he heard a voice saying, 'Vengeance, vengeance,' and saw a bird hovering above him as if beckoning him to follow. So he did follow the bird, and they went out of the palace and up to the top of a hill. While wandering there, he lost his way, and it was not until daybreak that he was able to start looking for the path again. When he turned towards the palace all he could see was a large lake, and his harp floating on the water.

The lake was said to be bottomless, and also to dislike anyone trying to find the bottom. When a man took a boat out to what was considered the deepest part, and threw out a plummet on a line, a loud voice cried from the water, 'Line cannot fathom me. Go, or I will swallow you up!' On another occasion, a diver who tried to find the bottom saw a dragon coiled up on the lake bed. Maybe dragons don't live there, but in recent years people have reported seeing something strange in the water. A woman being driven past the lake in October 1979 saw a humpbacked creature briefly emerge from foaming water. She discovered that the lake warden had also seen a humpbacked creature, and the local greengrocer had seen something while in a boat fishing. 'It had a large head like a football and rather big eyes . . . the body . . .was nearly 8 feet long. It wasn't aggressive at all. It swam towards us to within a few yards and then turned and disappeared.'

Bala is 17 miles north-east of Dolgellau, and the lake lies to the east of the main road between the two towns. It is possible to drive all the way round the lake, and there are numerous access points to the shore. Water sports are also available, and there is a narrow-gauge railway along the eastern shore.

••••••••••••••••••••••••••••••••••

Huw Lloyd's Pulpit, Ffestiniog

A natural column of rock in the middle of the River Cynfal is said to be the place where a seventeenth-century prophet, poet and wizard used to call up the dead. He also put curses on people who annoyed him. Before he died he requested that all his books of magic be thrown into Llyn Pont Rhydden, and a hand came out of the water to take them, in the same way that King Arthur's sword Excalibur was taken underwater.

The River Cynfal and its waterfall are just south of Ffestiniog, and reached along a signposted trackway to the left of the chapel. (SH 701413)

••••••••••••••••••••••••••••••••••

Llyn Cynwch

This is one of the lakes whose spirit periodically claims a victim. It was believed that on New Year's Eve, a person was seen walking back and forth along the lake shore, crying out in Welsh: 'The hour is come but not the man!' But there was one man who went into the lake and came out alive. He was a servant at Nannau, the big house near by, who one day fell into the lake, but didn't drown. As he sank, he found the water getting clearer and clearer, until he landed on the bottom and found people and places just as they were on dry land. A short fat old man asked him what he was doing there, and he was welcomed to the place. He stayed there a month, though it seemed like three days, and

his hosts then took him along an underground passage which led up under the hearthstone of another local house where his sweetheart worked. A deadly viper or serpent once lived by the lake: any living creature which was caught by its eye became helpless. A shepherd found it asleep, fetched an axe, and killed it. A cairn of stones was piled over its carcase, and the cairn is still known as Carnedd y Wiber.

Today the lake is along the route of the 3¹/₂ mile Precipice Walk, which is not difficult despite its name, and overlooks some beautiful views. The car park for the walk is 2¹/₂ miles north of Dolgellau, along the lane to Llanfachreth. (Car park OS map reference: SH 745211)

....

St Cybi's Chair (Cadair Gybi), Llangybi

One of numerous saint's chairs in Wales, this one is in a particularly atmospheric yet accessible location in woods just above the saint's holy well. The wooded hillside is steep and rocky and some exploration will be needed to locate the rock that is known as the saint's chair, but it is there.

The chair and well are at Llangybi on the Lleyn Peninsula, 5 miles north-east of Pwllheli. They are sited to the north-west of the village, reached by a footpath through the churchyard and into the valley. (SH 427414)

HEREFORDSHIRE

....

King Arthur's Cave

This cave was occupied from about 25,000 BC until Roman times, and archaeological excavation has uncovered the

bones of mammoths and other long-extinct species which were hunted by the earliest men who lived here. It is unlikely that King Arthur ever came here, but in folklore it was said that when he was hiding from his enemies he brought his treasure here for safe-keeping, and Merlin laid a spell on the cave so that the treasure would never be found.

The cave is not easy to find, being in woods on the north side of the River Wye and 1 mile south of Whitchurch (4 miles north-east of Monmouth), but a footpath leads to it from a lane south of the A40. (An Ordnance Survey map is essential, and the cave's map reference is SO 545155)

....

St Ethelbert's Well, Marden

This well is one of the few to be found inside a church. It is sited towards the rear of the nave, and is of course covered. It is said to mark the place where the body of the murdered King Ethelbert lay before being removed to Hereford, starting to flow after the body was taken away. The River Lugg close by the church is the place where an unsuccessful attempt was made, according to the story, to recover one of the church bells which had been lost in the river and was held captive by a mermaid. In fact in 1848 an ancient bronze handbell of the type used in the Celtic Church was discovered in a pond at Marden, lying at a depth of 18 feet under many centuries of mud and rubbish.

Marden is 4 miles north of Hereford.

INVERNESS

....

Loch Ness

The loch is 24 miles long and about 1 mile wide; it is also very deep, though exactly how deep is not known. According to legend, it was formed when the covering stone was left off a local well by a woman who heard her child crying and ran to it. The well overflowed and quickly filled the long valley. The people who lived there ran to the hills, crying, 'Tha loch nis ann, tha loch nis ann' (There is a loch there now) – hence its name. Alternatively the name came from the daughter of a giantess who drowned in the lake, or from an Irish hero called Nysus.

Loch Ness is best known for its monster, Nessie, which may or may not exist: neither sceptics nor believers have yet been able to prove their case. Sighting reports are said to go back to the seventh century, when St Adamnan, Abbot of Iona, wrote in his *Life of St Columba* about the saint's visit to the loch, where he saw a man who had died after being bitten by a water monster when swimming. The monster reappeared when one of the saint's companions dived into the loch to fetch a boat, and the saint made the sign of the cross over it and told it to stay in its lair, at which it fled. There is also a story that St Columba encountered the water-horse of the loch, but this creature was helpful and friendly, pulling the boats of the saint's party across the water, for which assistance St Columba blessed him and gave him the freedom of Loch Ness for ever. So it is unlikely that the two monsters were one and the same, though the water-horse did later make a pact with the Devil. This came about because the River Ness ran through the loch, and water-horses cannot cross running water, so he was worried about being unable to pass from one side of the loch to the other. The Devil told him that if he would give him one ride every year over any water he (the Devil) chose, he would ensure that the river flowed strictly along its ordained route and not mingle with the loch water, so

143

that the water-horse would be able to dive under it. In fact, although he did not know it, this happened anyway, so the Devil took advantage of the water-horse.

The folklorist Otta Swire wrote of hearing when she was a child of something evil living in the loch, of sacrifices of cattle made to it, of people drowning and their bodies never being found. It was said to have an outlet to the sea, and caverns where slimy, white, eyeless monsters lived. The woods around the loch were also haunted, one ghost being known as the Old Man of Inverfarigaig. Just along the shore is Boleskine House, where the notorious magician Aleister Crowley lived for a while, and it is possible that his magical practices could have helped to reinforce the evil atmosphere believed to lurk in the valley of Loch Ness. In 1973 the Reverend Dr Donald Omand attempted to exorcize the spirit of evil around Loch Ness.

Loch Ness is south-west of Inverness, and a road runs close to the shore for almost the whole of its length.

....

Tom-na-hurich Hill

This legendary fairy hill is almost swallowed up by the modern world, now that it is on the south-west outskirts of Inverness and has at its foot a modern cemetery and a main road; but nevertheless it retains something of its earlier magic. For this, the Hill of the Yews, was a fairy dwelling ruled by a fairy queen, who once decided she wanted a young, handsome piper who had taken her fancy. He was brought to her, and she told him she intended to make him her consort, but he refused the honour, because he wished to return to his wife and child in Inverness. The Queen said he would never find them again, but he still refused to marry her, or to eat fairy food, and so they let him go. Arriving home, he found that his family had been taken away, but one of the fairies who felt sorry for him told him to go to the hill and sing a certain song which she taught him. He did

so, and his wife and baby son were pushed out of the door in the hill that led to the fairy dwelling.

Several hundred years ago, two fiddlers were taken into the hill to play for a dance. At dawn, they were paid and went home. But they found the town very much changed, and when they told an old man where they had been, he said he remembered his grandfather telling him of two young fiddlers who had vanished when he was a boy, a hundred years before. He showed them what they looked like in a mirror, and they saw two old men with long white beards. They were frightened and went into church, a familiar place, but when the Minister pronounced the blessing they both crumbled into dust. What seemed to them only a night had in human time been a hundred years or more.

Thomas the Rhymer, or alternatively Fionn (King of the Feinn) and his men, lie sleeping in the hill, so it is said. Thomas comes out from time to time to buy special horses for his warriors, who are also waiting inside the hill for the time when a great battle will be fought.

The Brahan Seer, who was born around 1600 and was famous in Scotland as a prophet, predicted that ships with unfurled sails would pass and repass Tom-na-hurich, and that it would be placed under lock and key. The opening of the Caledonian Canal which passes alongside the hill was the fulfilment of the first part of the prophecy; the development of the cemetery is seen as the second part.

The hill is a mile to the south-west of the centre of Inverness, and to the west of the A82.

LANCASHIRE

....

Pendle Hill

The Forest of Pendle, Pendle Hill, and the whole area around Newchurch-in-Pendle has been famous for almost 300

years as a hotbed of witchcraft. In 1612 a total of nineteen witches were tried at Lancaster, nine were found not guilty, one known as Old Demdike had died in prison, one was sentenced to the pillory, and the remaining eight were hanged. A further group stood trial in 1633. A book was written about the 1612 case, *A Wonderfulle Discoverie of Witches in the County of Lancaster* by Thomas Potts, which gives details of the witches' confessions. But as is usual in such cases, it is likely that much of the evidence against the women was fabricated, and that they confessed under pressure.

There are still some reminders of Pendle's notorious history to be found today. At St Mary's church, Newchurch, an eye made of stone and slate is visible on the side of the tower, put there to protect the church and its congregation against the witches' evil eye. In the churchyard, close to the church door, is the grave of one of the women who was supposedly a witch, Alice Nutter. On the Lamb Inn near the church two witch figures decorate the front wall, and other witch symbols can be seen round about.

Newchurch is approximately 4 miles north of Burnley.

MID GLAMORGAN

....

Kenfig Pool

There was once an important Norman castle at Kenfig, and a medieval town, but from the thirteenth century the whole area was gradually engulfed by sand, so that today there is only Kenfig Burrows, an area of coastal sand dunes, and Kenfig Pool. Naturally the legendary explanation for the disappearance of Kenfig is much more dramatic. A local chieftain injured a prince, who with his dying breath laid a curse on the chieftain. Some time later, long after the curse had been forgotten, a voice was

heard crying 'Vengeance is coming!' But this too was ignored, and the chieftain's descendants held a grand feast. The warning cry continued to ring out, and then water rushed into the palace. No one could escape, and all of Kenfig was drowned. Another version of the story tells how a poor peasant's son killed a man and stole his money so that he could marry the daughter of a lord. The voice cried vengeance, and when asked when it would happen, the voice said 'At the end of the ninth generation', and so it happened. Crymlyn Pool further along the coast is said to cover the old town of Swansea.

Kenfig Burrows and Pool now form a nature reserve, as the area is very rich in birdlife and plants. It is open to the public, and there are some fine walks through the dunes to the seashore. Kenfig is 3 miles north of Porthcawl.

NORFOLK

....

St Withburga's Well, East Dereham

This well is easy to find, being situated in the churchyard and on the west side of St Nicholas's church. It is well maintained, and marks the spot where the saint's body was buried before being stolen and taken away to Ely in 974. The remains of the walls of a chapel which once stood over the well can still be seen, but there are no signs of the bath-house which was built in the late eighteenth century.

East Dereham is 14 miles west of Norwich.

NORTHUMBERLAND

••••••••••••••••••••••••••••

Drake Stone and Harbottle Lough

This 30-foot stone in the Harbottle Hills was said to have
been the site for 'Druidic rites', but it was best known as a
place where sick children could be cured. The procedure was to
pass them over the top of the stone, which must have been nerve-
racking for all concerned. Beyond the stone is Harbottle Lough,
a lonely stretch of water with a guardian who protested when
workmen started to drain it. A voice from the depths said:

> *'Let alone, let alone!*
> *Or a'll droon Harbottle an' the Peels*
> *An' the bonny Hallystone.'*

Harbottle is 16 miles south-west of Alnwick, and a footpath at
West Wood leads up into the hills. The Drake Stone is clearly
visible at the top of the slope; the lough is a short distance further
on. (NT 920044)

••••••••••••••••••••••••••••

St Cuthbert's Cave

Also known as Cuddie's Cave or Cuddy's Cove, this impressive cave has two links with St Cuthbert, the monk who was
bishop of Lindisfarne in the seventh century. He is said to have
lived here as a hermit, and also that this was one of the resting-
places when his body was being carried from Lindisfarne to
Durham after the Vikings raided Lindisfarne. The cave was
believed to be haunted by the Hazelrigg Dunny, the ghost of a
reiver or raider who had buried his treasure somewhere in
Bowden Doors, a rocky. area to the south, and had then 'lost the
keys'. He was called a Dunny because he sometimes appeared in
the form of a dun-coloured horse, and he used to annoy the

people of Hazelrigg nearby. A very strange saying about the cave was that it was here that the Devil hanged his granny!

Situated well off the beaten track, in woods on Cockenheugh a mile north of Hazelrigg (5 miles north-east of Wooler), the cave is in the care of the National Trust and reached by footpath from a car park at Holburn Grange. (NU 058352)

NORTH YORKSHIRE

....

Brimham Rocks

The natural forces of ice and frost, wind and rain, have eroded the millstone grit over thousands of years into all kinds of weird formations and man has given them appropriate names, such as Chimney Rock, Baboon, Dancing Bear, Yoke of Oxen. From the belief that strange rituals were practised here have come names such as Druid's Skull and Druid's Altar.

The rocks are on 50 acres of moorland overlooking Nidderdale, 8 miles south-west of Ripon, and the site is in the care of the National Trust.

....

Mother Shipton's Cave and the Petrifying Well, Knaresborough

Mother Shipton, who became a famous prophetess, was said to have been born in this cave in 1488, fifteen years before Nostradamus. Some of her prophecies were faked in the last century, but she is definitely supposed to have prophesied that 'The world shall end when the High Bridge is thrice fallen.' This refers to a bridge over the River Nidd in Knaresborough, not far

from the cave. It has fallen twice already! A scenic walk through woods along the riverbank leads to the cave, which can be entered. Close to it is the amazing Dripping Well, also known as the Petrifying Well because of the way it turns to stone any object left within the flow of water over the rock. There is also a separate wishing well under the rocks behind the Dripping Well.

Knaresborough is 3 miles north-east of Harrogate, and the well and Mother Shipton's Cave are signposted in the town. They are located in a park with ample parking, picnic areas by the river, cafe, museum, shop, etc., but a sizable admission charge is payable.

OXFORDSHIRE

Dragon Hill, Uffington

Although the chalk hill figure on the slope above Dragon Hill is known as the Uffington White Horse, the name 'Dragon Hill' indicates that in legend at least, he has a dual role as a dragon. The figure is thought to date from the Iron Age, and may be the oldest hill figure in Britain. Dragon Hill has a flat top, and it was here that St George slew the dragon, the white patch of bare chalk marking the place where its poisonous blood fell. The dragon itself may lie buried under the hill. The hill figure can only be viewed in its entirety from a distance, or from the air, but you can walk across the hill and stand above it, looking down onto Dragon Hill in the valley below.

The White Horse and Dragon Hill are 1½ miles south of Uffington village, itself 6 miles north-west of Wantage, and reached along a lane off the B4507.

PERTH

••••••••••••••••••••••••••••••••••••

Fairy Hill, Aberfoyle

Robert Kirk was the Presbyterian minister at Aberfoyle who in the late seventeenth century wrote a book about fairies, *The Secret Common-Wealth*. When he died while walking on the Fairy Hill close to his home, on 14 May 1692 at the age of forty-eight, it was believed that he had not died but had been taken into Fairyland through the door on the hill. It was also said that he appeared to a relative and told him that he could be rescued from Fairyland. This could be brought about if his cousin were to throw a knife over Kirk's apparition when it appeared at the christening of his posthumous child, thereby breaking the spell that held him – because iron has power over the fairies. As promised, Kirk appeared at the christening, but his cousin was too amazed to remember to throw the knife, and Kirk was never seen again. His grave can still be seen in the old burial ground, but it was believed that his body was not there, and that the coffin was full of stones.

Aberfoyle is 8 miles south-west of Callander, and the old burial ground is at Kirkton to the south-west. Kirk's grave is covered by a horizontal slab and has a Latin inscription: it is at the corner of the ruined building. The lane past the burial ground leads on to the Fairy Hill, where a walk up the hill is waymarked. It is still a magical place, and it is possible that a psychic person would be able to sense the fairies there, even today.

POWYS

....

Llangorse Lake

Also known as Llyn Safaddan, Brecknock Mere, Talyllyn Pool, and Lake of Brycheiniog, the water is said to cover a city which was swallowed up by an earthquake. This happened in vengeance for a murder. A man killed another man for his money, so that he could marry a princess, but she felt uneasy because the dead man's ghost was haunting his grave. So she sent her admirer to lay the ghost, and he heard a voice asking whether the innocent man was not to be avenged, and another replying that he would be avenged at the ninth generation. Thus reassured, the couple married and had children, and their town grew in size and in evil practices. The pair lived so long that they were celebrating their prosperity with a great banquet which was attended by all their descendants down to the ninth generation. At the height of the celebrations, a mighty cataclysm overwhelmed the town and all the people living there. Centuries later it was still believed that the bells of the drowned church could be heard ringing in rough weather, and that the church spire could be seen in calm weather. The remains of a prehistoric lake dwelling have been found at the north end of the lake, and possibly the memory of this ancient settlement may have suggested the story of the drowned town.

Llangorse Lake is 5 miles south-east of Brecon.

ROSS AND CROMARTY

....

Loch Garve

Many Highland lochs have tales of strange occupants, but this is one of the most amusing. It is the story of a water-

horse who couldn't find a wife. Being cold-blooded, they never feel the cold, nor do they like eating cooked food, preferring raw fish or raw waterweed and water-snails. Sometimes they carry off girls to be their wives, and they try their best to keep them happy, because water-horses are by and large kindly creatures. They build underwater houses, and catch plenty of fresh fish. But the girl who had been taken by the Loch Garve water-horse was still not happy. One day as he returned home he heard her crying 'I'm so cold, so cold.' So the water-horse went into the village of Garve and, in his guise of a land-horse, he searched for the mason. This man took the horse's bridle and got on his back, thinking of course that he was a real horse, and so he was rather frightened when the water-horse began to gallop back to the loch. But he persuaded him to build a fireplace with a chimney, and then he took him back home. Now his wife is warm and happy, and can eat her fish fried. Until his death the mason only had to go to the lochside and say 'Fish', and next day he would find a basket of fish waiting for him on a certain boulder. But someone else who tried this after the mason's death came to a bad end. There is at the eastern end of the loch a patch of water that never freezes, even though the rest of the surface may be frozen. Even though it is probably an underwater spring which keeps the water clear, it is nicer to think that it is the chimney of the water-horse's house.

Loch Garve is 4 miles west of Strathpeffer, and the A832 road runs along the southern shore.

ROXBURGH

....

Eildon Hills

It was the wizard Michael Scot who changed the shape of Eildon from one hill into three. A thirteenth-century scholar,

Michael Scot's interest in science and astrology gained him a reputation as a magician, but there is no proof that he actually practised magic, and in his writings he condemned it. Other acts of magic in the area of northern England and southern Scotland have been credited to him: he built Hadrian's Wall with the Devil's help, for example. One of the places where he is said to be buried is Melrose Abbey close by the Eildon Hills.

It was somewhere in the Eildon Hills that Thomas the Rhymer (Thomas of Erceldoune) met the Fairy Queen. When he first saw her riding by, as he lay on the ground, he thought she was the Queen of Heaven, but she said she came from another country. He persuaded her to make love with him, but afterwards she had power over him, and made him go with her under the hills, where they wandered for three days and nights. She led him to Fairyland, where he lived for three years, though it seemed like only three days. Then she took him back out of Fairyland, and left him with an inability to tell a lie, and a knowledge of the future.

There was also a legend that Thomas is sleeping inside the hills, coming out periodically to buy horses for his warriors who with him await the call to battle. A horse-seller called Canonbie Dick was riding over the hills with two horses he had not been able to sell, when he met an old man who said he would buy both of them, and to bring more to the same place. On one occasion when he did so, he was taken into the hills through a passage at the foot of a small hill called the Lucken Hare, and in a cave he saw stables full of black horses, and sleeping knights, and a table on which lay a horn and a sword. Thomas of Erceldoune, for he was the old man, said that Dick could become King of Britain if he drew the sword and blew the horn – but in the right order. So he blew the horn and tried to lift the heavy sword, but a loud voice then said:

> '*Woe to the coward that ever he was born,*
> *Who did not draw the sword before he blew the horn.*'

And Dick was carried out of the cave on a whirlwind. He was

found by some shepherds, and lived just long enough to tell them what had happened to him.

There are many sites in Britain where, according to folklore, hero figures are lying asleep, waiting until they are needed to help their country, and the identification of the hero varies from place to place. The men asleep in the Eildon Hills have also been identified as King Arthur and his knights.

The Eildon Hills are just south of Melrose, and 3 miles east of Galashiels. The 4-mile Eildon Walk is a circular route through the hills, beginning and ending at Melrose.

SHROPSHIRE

·······································

Colemere

This is one of several meres around Ellesmere in north Shropshire. It is said to conceal a drowned monastery which previously stood here before a spring overflowed and formed the lake. The chapel bells can be heard on windy nights at full moon, or so it was said. An alternative story is that a chapel on the banks of the lake was pulled down and the bells thrown into the water. There is some evidence that there was indeed once a chapel beside Colemere. According to legend, there was once an attempt to lift the bells. Chains had been attached to them and twenty oxen managed to bring them to the shore, but then one of the workmen said, 'In spite of God and the Devil . . . we have done it!', whereupon the chains snapped and the bells rolled back into the water.

Colemere is 2 miles south-east of Ellesmere, and just north of Colemere village. A footpath follows the westerly edge, and the northern edge of the lake is bounded by the Shropshire Union Canal, from which Colemere can be glimpsed through the trees.

....

The Mere, Ellesmere

A fearsome hag was said to dwell in the lake: Jenny Greenteeth, who hides under the waterweed and will stretch out her long arms to grab any children who venture too near to the water. Where the lake now stands, used to be meadowland with a well in the middle which supplied a great many people. But the owners of the land were mean, and charged a halfpenny for each bucket of water. The poor people prayed to the Almighty for help, and the well overflowed and flooded all the land, so that there was free water for all. In one version the water came from a pump owned by a Mrs Ellis, who would not sell or give any water to her neighbours. When the well overflowed, neither she nor her pump were ever seen again, and the resulting lake was called Ellesmere after her.

The Mere is on the eastern side of Ellesmere town, and the A528 road to Shrewsbury passes by it. There is roadside parking, and easy access to the water, which is rich in birdlife.

....

The Stiperstones

A rocky ridge near the Welsh border, the Stiperstones 'rears its long fish-shaped back, crowned by a row of five curious projecting rocks, which from a distance look as if they might be the huge fins of some primaeval monster', in the words of the folklorist Charlotte S. Burne. The highest of these rocks is known as the Devil's Chair, after he used it as a resting-place when on his way from Ireland with an apronful of stones. As he got up to continue his journey (no one is quite sure where he was going), his apron-string broke and all the stones scattered on to the ground around his chair, where they still lie. The local people even believed that you could still smell the brimstone!

According to another tale, the Devil sits on his chair hoping to push the rocks back into the ground, and so fulfil the prophecy that when the Stiperstones sink into the earth, England will be ruined. One day the Devil found a giantess trying to carry his chair away, and so he cut her apron-strings and she dropped the load of stones she was carrying, forming a cairn on the ridge.

The Stiperstones are 6 miles north-east of Bishop's Castle and run for 1¹/₂ miles to the south and east of the village of Pennerley. There is a footpath along the ridge, starting at the car park at the southern end, on the lane between Ratlinghope and Pennerley, though the rocky terrain makes for difficult walking.

....

The Wrekin

The Wrekin, 1,334 feet high, stands prominently above the surrounding flat plain, looking decidedly out of place, and folklore explains how the hill came to be there. There are two versions. In one, a giant with a grudge against Shrewsbury was carrying a load of earth with which to bury the town. He met a cobbler on the road and asked him the way. Realizing what the giant intended to do, the cobbler showed him the bag of boots he was carrying and told him that he had worn them all out since leaving Shrewsbury. Disheartened by the long journey apparently still ahead of him, the giant dumped his load of earth, forming the Wrekin. The soil he scraped from his boots formed the neighbouring Ercall Hill.

In the alternative story, two giants constructed the Wrekin as a safe place to live, using earth they dug from the bed of the nearby River Severn. Traces of their presence can still be seen: bare patches on the hill are said to be their footprints; while the Needle's Eye, a cleft rock on the summit, was formed as the result of a quarrel between the two giants. One hit out at the other with his spade, missed, and split the rock. The attacking giant was himself attacked by the other's pet raven, which

pecked out his eyes. The tears he shed fell into a rock basin, now called the Raven's Bowl, still to be seen on the summit and supposedly always full of water. The blinded giant was overpowered by his former friend and imprisoned in Ercall Hill, from where his groans can still be heard at dead of night.

The Raven's Bowl was also known as the Cuckoo's Cup, and in another tale was said to have been miraculously formed as a drinking place for those birds. It was, at one time, the custom for visitors to the Wrekin to taste the water in the hollow, a ritual surviving, possibly, from the ancient Wrekin Wake, a festival formerly held on the first Sunday in May. The top of the hill would be covered by 'ale-booths, ginger-bread-standings, gaming tables, swing-boats, merry-go-rounds, three-sticks-a-penny, and all the etceteras of an old English fair'. In addition, a battle was held between the colliers and the countrymen for possession of the hill. This sometimes resulted in fatalities, so fierce was the fighting, and as a result the wake was done away with.

The Wrekin is 9 miles south-east of Shrewsbury, and a good, if steep, footpath to the summit starts at the north-east where a lane passes between the Wrekin and Ercall Hill.

SOMERSET

....

Glastonbury Tor and Chalice Well

Glastonbury Tor is a prominent and powerful hill which dominates the countryside around Glastonbury. On top is the tower of St Michael's church (the rest of the building fell in a thirteenth-century earthquake), and all around the hill can be seen terraces which may indicate a processional way or some form of labyrinthine path leading up the hill. This is the place where St Collen encountered Gwyn, the fairy king, inside his

Fairyland castle, but believing them to be demons, he scattered holy water all around, and found himself alone on the hillside. There is a local tradition that the Holy Grail was hidden at the base of the Tor in Chalice Well, also known as Blood Spring because of the reddish colour of the water. The well is now to be found in a peaceful garden which is open to visitors, on payment of a small admission charge (*see plate 12*).

The Tor lies just to the east of Glastonbury, and north of the A361 to Shepton Mallet. There are two public paths up the hill, both starting in Well House Lane.

SUFFOLK

....

Druid's Stone

Alternative names for this 3 feet high rounded stone in St Mary's churchyard in Bungay are Devil's Stone and Giant's Grave. It may be a glacial erratic. It was believed that if you ran around it twelve times, or knocked on it twelve times, and placed your ear to the stone, you would hear the answers to your questions or wishes. Or else that dancing round it seven times on a certain day would summon up the Devil.

It was in this same church, in 1577, that the Devil in the form of a black dog wrought havoc among the congregation when he passed through, killing some and injuring others. The true cause may have been ball lightning or some other rare natural phenomenon. There is now a black dog weathervane in the town centre commemorating this event.

Bungay is 12 miles west of Lowestoft, and St Mary's church is in the town centre.

SUTHERLAND

....

Smoo Cave

A dramatic cave consisting of three chambers, the first 200 feet long and 120 feet high, with a 53 foot high entrance, it was here that a seventeenth-century wizard, Lord Reay, had an encounter with the Devil. They had first met in Padua, where Lord Reay had joined a school for students of the Black Arts which the Devil had just opened. Lord Reay lost his shadow to the Devil when he outwitted him into taking only his shadow rather than himself, and the Devil pursued him when he returned to Scotland. They had a fist-fight on the moors, which Lord Reay won. They became good friends, but the Devil had lost face in the fight and wanted to get his revenge. One day when Lord Reay went to explore Smoo Cave, the Devil found out and got there first. Lord Reay's dog went ahead of him into the third cavern, and returned 'howling and hairless', so Lord Reay knew who was waiting for him. He immediately set his mind to defeating the Devil, but while he was working out his scheme the cock crew and the Devil, together with the three witches who had come with him, realized that he had to escape quickly, so they blew holes in the cavern roof through which to escape, rather than having to face Lord Reay in the outer chambers. Now the water of Smoo Burn enters the caverns through these holes.

Another version tells how, on his return to Scotland, Lord Reay met the Devil at Smoo Cave and they fought there, Lord Reay being the loser. He escaped on his horse and the hoofmarks can still be seen by the entrance to the cave. Later, he went into Smoo Cave to explore every inch of it, and deep inside he found a cask. He cut a hole into the cask with his knife, and a tiny man only 1¹/₂ inches tall popped out. Initially surprised, Lord Reay became frightened as the little man began to grow rapidly, saying to Lord Reay as he did so: 'Did you ever behold a greater wonder?' Lord Reay replied: 'Never in all my life, but it would be

a greater wonder still if you could become a wee man again!' At

which the giant began to get smaller, and eventually he slipped back into the hole, which Lord Reay quickly plugged.

2 miles east of Durness on the north coast.

WEST GLAMORGAN

••••••••••••••••••••••••••••••••••••••

Craig-y-Ddinas

This rocky outcrop was said to be one of the last strongholds of the fairies in Wales (*see plate 3*). It is also one of the places where King Arthur and his men lie sleeping (or alternatively it is the Welsh hero Owen Lawgoch). There is also treasure in the cave with the sleeping men. Traditionally, a magician showed the cave to a man who was allowed to take some of the gold, and told that if he rang the bell, one of the knights would awake and ask if it was day. He was supposed to answer: 'No, sleep on.' When he knocked the bell by accident, it rang and the knight awoke. The correct answer was given on this occasion, but on a later visit, he again rang the bell but forgot the right answer. The warriors beat him savagely, and took back the gold. He could never find the place again. Unlike other places of folklore which have been spoilt by the encroachment of modern dwellings and other signs of 'civilization', Craig-y-Ddinas is still a magical place, in its setting of wood and water. Visit it at the right time – dawn, dusk, or when there is a full moon, for example – when there is no one else around, and the spirit of the place cannot fail to touch you.

Craig-y-Ddinas is close to the River Neath in the Vale of Neath just east of Pontneddfechan, north of the A465; there is car parking, and woodland walks.

161

....

Worm's Head, Gower

The views from the headland at the far tip of the Gower Peninsula in South Wales are breathtaking, with the vast beach at Rhossili stretching away below you, and the sinuous Worm's Head projecting into the sea behind you (*see plate 24*). This headland's resemblance to a sea-serpent is striking, and in stormy weather when the spray leaps up from the blowhole on the Outer Head, a strange booming sound makes the Worm seem like a living creature. The old Gower fishermen used to say: 'The old Worm's blowing, time for a boat to be going.' At high tide the Worm is an island, so explorers should remember that they only have about five hours on the Worm. There are three sections, Inner, Middle and Outer Head, the last two being linked by a huge natural limestone arch called the Devil's Bridge. At the end of the headland there is a sheer 100-foot drop from the clifftop into the sea. In a cave about 15 feet above the high-water mark, bones of mammoth, rhinoceros, reindeer and cave bear were found, and a passage leads deep into the rock. An underground passage is said to lead to Worm's Head from a Carmarthenshire valley. Today the Head is a nature reserve.

Worm's Head is off the south-west tip of the Gower Peninsula, 15 miles from Swansea, and the nearest village is Rhossili, where there are car parking and other facilities.

Bibliography

These books were our major sources and are recommended for further reading.

Ashe, Geoffrey, *A Guidebook to Arthurian Britain*, Longman, 1980

Bell, David, *Leicestershire Ghosts and Legends*, Countryside Books, 1992

Boase, Wendy, *The Folklore of Hampshire and the Isle of Wight*, B.T. Batsford, 1976

Bord, Janet and Colin, *Atlas of Magical Britain*, Sidgwick & Jackson, 1990

Bord, Janet and Colin, *Sacred Waters: Holy Wells and Water Lore in Britain and Ireland*, Granada Publishing, 1985

Bord, Janet and Colin, *The Secret Country: An Interpretation of the Folklore of Ancient Sites in the British Isles*, Paul Elek, 1976; Paladin/Granada Publishing, 1978

Brockie, William, *Legends and Superstitions of the County of Durham*, 1886; republished by EP Publishing, 1974

Burne, Charlotte Sophia, *Shropshire Folk-Lore*, Trübner & Co., 1883; republished by EP Publishing, 1973

Clarke, David, and Rob Wilson, *Strange Sheffield*, ASSAP, 1987

Davies, Jonathan Ceredig, *Folk-Lore of West and Mid-Wales*, 1911; republished by Llanerch Publishers, 1992

Deane, Tony, and Tony Shaw, *The Folklore of Cornwall*, B.T. Batsford, 1975

Gould, Jack, *Gothick Northamptonshire*, Shire Publications, 1992

Gray, Affleck, *Legends of the Cairngorms*, Mainstream Publishing, 1987

Harland, John, and T.T. Wilkinson, *Lancashire Folk-Lore*, John Heywood, 1882; republished by EP Publishing, 1973

Hole, Christina, *Traditions and Customs of Cheshire*, Williams and Norgate, 1937; republished by S.R. Publishers, 1970

Holland, Richard, *Supernatural Clwyd*, Gwasg Carreg Gwalch, 1989

Hunt, Robert, *Popular Romances of the West of England*, 1871; republished by Llanerch Publishers, 1993

Jones, T. Gwynn, *Welsh Folklore and Folk-Custom*, 1930; republished by D.S. Brewer, 1979

Jones-Baker, Doris, *The Folklore of Hertfordshire*, B.T. Batsford, 1977

Killip, Margaret, *The Folklore of the Isle of Man*, B.T. Batsford, 1975

Leather, Ella Mary, *The Folk-Lore of Herefordshire*, Jakeman & Carver, 1912; republished by S.R. Publishers, 1970

MacGregor, Alasdair Alpin, *The Peat-Fire Flame*, The Moray Press, 1937

MacKenzie, Donald A., *Scottish Folk-Lore and Folk Life*, Blackie & Son, 1935

McPherson, J.M., *Primitive Beliefs in the North-East of Scotland*, Longmans, Green and Co., 1929

Marwick, Ernest W., *The Folklore of Orkney and Shetland*, B.T. Batsford, 1975

Moore, A.W., *The Folk-Lore of the Isle of Man*, D. Nutt, 1891; republished by S.R. Publishers, 1971

Nicolson, James R., *Shetland Folklore*, Robert Hale, 1981

Owen, Rev. Elias, *Welsh Folk-Lore*, Woodall Minshall & Co., 1888; republished by EP Publishing, 1976

Palmer, Kingsley, *The Folklore of Somerset*, B.T. Batsford, 1976

Palmer, Roy, *The Folklore of Hereford & Worcester*, Logaston Press, 1992

Palmer, Roy, *The Folklore of Warwickshire*, B.T. Batsford, 1976

Parry-Jones, D., *Welsh Legends and Fairy Lore*, B.T. Batsford, 1953

Porter, Enid, *The Folklore of East Anglia*, B.T. Batsford, 1974

Raven, Jon, *The Folklore of Staffordshire*, B.T. Batsford, 1978

Rhys, John, *Celtic Folklore, Welsh and Manx*, Oxford University Press, 1901; republished by Wildwood House, 1980

Roderick, Alan, *The Folklore of Glamorgan*, Village Publishing, 1986

Roderick, Alan, *The Folklore of Gwent*, Village Publishing, 1983

Ross, Anne, *The Folklore of the Scottish Highlands*, B.T. Batsford, 1976

Rowling, Marjorie, *The Folklore of the Lake District*, B.T. Batsford, 1976

Rudkin, Ethel H., *Lincolnshire Folklore*, Beltons, 1936; republished by EP Publishing, 1973

St Leger-Gordon, Ruth E., *The Witchcraft and Folklore of Dartmoor*, Robert Hale, 1965; republished by EP Publishing, 1973

Sikes, Wirt, *British Goblins*, Sampson Low, 1880; republished by EP Publishing, 1973

Simpson, Jacqueline, *The Folklore of Sussex*, B.T. Batsford, 1973

Simpson, Jacqueline, *The Folklore of the Welsh Border*, B.T. Batsford, 1976

Swire, Otta F., *The Highlands and Their Legends*, Oliver & Boyd, 1963

Swire, Otta F., *The Outer Hebrides and Their Legends*, Oliver & Boyd, 1966

Tongue, R.L., *Somerset Folklore*, The Folk-Lore Society, 1965

Trevelyan, Marie, *Folk-Lore and Folk-Stories of Wales*, 1909; republished by EP Publishing, 1973

Walker, Charles, *The Atlas of Occult Britain*, Hamlyn, 1987

Walker, Charles, *Strange Britain*, Brian Trodd Publishing House, 1989

Waring, Edward, *Ghosts and Legends of the Dorset Countryside*, Compton Press 1977

Westwood, Jennifer, *Albion: A Guide to Legendary Britain*, Granada Publishing, 1985

Westwood, Jennifer, *Gothick Cornwall*, Shire Publications, 1992

Westwood, Jennifer, *Gothick Hertfordshire*, Shire Publications, 1989

Westwood, Jennifer, *Gothick Norfolk*, Shire Publications, 1989

Whitlock, Ralph, *The Folklore of Devon*, B.T. Batsford, 1977

Whitlock Ralph, *The Folklore of Wiltshire*, B.T. Batsford, 1976

Whitworth, Belinda, *Gothick Devon*, Shire Publications, 1993

Williams, Guy, A *Guide to the Magical Places of England, Wales and Scotland*, Constable, 1987

Index

PLATE 24.
Worm's Head, a coastal headland on the
Gower peninsula in West Glamorgan, resembles
a giant dragon or serpent (they were once
called worms).

PLATE 23.
The topmost stone of the Cheesewring, high up on Bodmin Moor in Cornwall, was said to turn around three times when the cock crowed.

PLATE 21.
Above: The Storr Pinnacles on the
Isle of Skye, dominated by the Old
Man of Storr. He and his wife (now
fallen) were turned to stone by giants
while searching for a lost cow.

PLATE 22.
Right: The mysterious woods
on the sandstone cliff that is Alderley
Edge in Cheshire conceal caves where
King Arthur and his knights are said
to lie sleeping. Memories of Merlin
the magician also haunt the Edge,
especially at the Wizard's Well.

PLATE 20.
A fairy woman from Llyn-y-Fan-Fach in the
Black Mountains of Dyfed, who married a
human but later returned with her cattle to
her home in the lake.

PLATE 19.
The Mere at Ellesmere in Shropshire marks
the place where a well overflowed to drown
the owners of it, who were charging too
much for the water.

PLATE 18.
A standing stone resembling a woman stands
close to Grace's Well and a lake near Llangybi in
Gwynedd. In folklore it represents Grace, who
left the well open, so that it overflowed to form
the Lake Glasfryn.

The effigies of the Triton *and* Siren *of* Nilus.

PLATE 16.
Above: A 17th-century
drawing of a merman and
a mermaid, of whom there
have been numerous
sightings around Britain's
shores, according to folklore.

PLATE 17.
Right: The mermaid on
a bench-end in Zennor
church, Cornwall, commemorates the tale of a local lad
enticed away into the sea by
a mermaid.

PLATE 13.
Above left: Entranced by the fairy music, a man about to join the ring of dancing fairies is pulled back just in time. If he had joined the dance, he would have been unable to leave of his own free will.

PLATE 14.
Left: St Michael's Mount, a famous Cornish landmark, was said to have been built by giants. It was once surrounded by trees: Mount's Bay is a submerged forest.

PLATE 15.
Above: The calm seashore conceals a turbulent past at Dunwich in Suffolk where a once bustling seaport has been swallowed up by the sea. Some say that the bells of drowned churches can be heard ringing to warn of storms.

PLATE 11.
Left: This carving in Hennock church, Devon, depicts St Sidwell who was beheaded in the 8th century on the order of her jealous stepmother.

PLATE 12.
Below: Chalice Well, below the Tor in Glastonbury, Somerset, is one of the places where the Holy Grail was said to be hidden: the reddish water (caused by the presence of iron) reminded people of blood.

PLATE 10.
St Winefride's Well, Holywell, Clwyd: in the
foreground the spring bubbles up, flowing outside
into a large bathing pool. Many pilgrims still visit
the well, which began to flow at the spot where
St Winefride's head fell when she was decapitated
by a rejected suitor.

PLATE 9.
One of the seven wonders of Wales, Pistyll
Rhaeadr waterfall on the Powys/Clwyd border
was said to be the home of a winged serpent.

PLATE 6.
The fearsome Kelpie,
water-horse of Scottish legend,
gloats over yet another
hapless victim.

PLATE 7.
The folk hero Guy, Earl of
Warwick, slaying a giant boar,
in an illustration from an
18th century chapbook.

PLATE 8.
Mother Shipton was a famous
16th century prophetess from
Knaresborough in North
Yorkshire, where her cave can
still be visited.

PLATE 3.
Left: Craig-y-Ddinas in the Vale of Neath
(West Glamorgan) is a magical place: not only
is it a fairy site, but one of the places where
King Arthur and his men are said to
lie sleeping.

PLATE 4.
Below left: This memorial near Dunning
(Perth) reminds us of the tragic fate that befell
so many innocent women during the witch
hunts in the Middle Ages.

PLATE 5.
Below: Caerphilly Castle in Mid Glamorgan,
haunted by a ghostly river hag with bat-like
wings and long black hair.

PLATE 1.
Suilven in Sutherland, one of the Scottish mountains said to
have been shaped by the giant hands of Norse gods.

PLATE 2.
Fairies dancing, close to a bushy mound with a doorway
which is presumably an entrance to Fairyland.